WHAT PEOF

DREAMS AI

Because most of us do not think too seriously about such things as eternal life, nor do we think in a dispassionate way, I cannot imagine that anyone would not profit from reading this well-reasoned, but also 'faith-filled" study about our life beyond this life. Read and be energized!
Fr. Richard Rohr, O.F.M., Center for Action and Contemplation, Albuquerque, New Mexico

. . . wonderfully, exhilaratingly, and convincingly interesting. . . . I'm so glad I spent time with this book. Not only was it intellectually engaging, it shifted some of my own thinking regarding life after death, and more to the point, about what it means to be a human being. And so I say to my friends and colleagues: Buckle up. Enjoy the ride. Prepare to see yourself (and everyone around you) in a new way!
Rev. Dr. R. Scott Colglazier, Senior Minister, First Congregational Church of Los Angeles, author of *A Dictionary of Faith*

A fascinating personal argument for the reality of eternal life and its relationship with Christianity, using the rigorous approach of the western philosophical tradition, spiced with the author's psychedelic experiences as a young man. Highly recommended.
Simon Small, Priest, author of *From the Bottom of the Pond* and *Star Pilgrim*, Glastonbury, UK

Dreams and Resurrection joins a celebrated history of important philosophical works dedicated to exploring the concepts of death and immortality. In the tradition of great public intellectuals such as Alan Watts and Jiddu Krishnamurti, Jack Call makes a very difficult topic accessible to the non-academic reader without sacrificing the standards of academic, intellectual rigor.

Kurt Smith, Philosophy Professor, Bloomsburg University of Pennsylvania

Dreams
and Resurrection

On Immortal Selves, Psychedelics,
and Christianity

Dreams
and Resurrection

On Immortal Selves, Psychedelics,
and Christianity

Jack Call

CHRISTIAN
ALTERNATIVE

Winchester, UK
Washington, USA

First published by Christian Alternative Books, 2014
Christian Alternative Books is an imprint of John Hunt Publishing Ltd.,
Laurel House, Station Approach,
Alresford, Hants, SO24 9JH, UK
office1@jhpbooks.net
www.johnhuntpublishing.com
www.christian-alternative.com

For distributor details and how to order please visit the 'Ordering' section on our website.

Text copyright: Jack Call 2013

ISBN: 978 1 78279 683 1

A CIP catalogue record for this book is available from the British Library.

Design: Stuart Davies

Printed and bound by CPI Group (UK) Ltd, Croydon, CR0 4YY

We operate a distinctive and ethical publishing philosophy in all
areas of our business, from our global network of authors to
production and worldwide distribution.

CONTENTS

God in His infinite goodness gives being to all in the way in which each can receive it. With Him there is no jealousy. He communicates being without distinction; and, since all receive being in accord with the demands of their contingent nature, every creature rests content in its own perfection, which God has freely bestowed upon it. None desires the greater perfection of any other; each loves by preference that perfection which God has given it and strives to develop and preserve it intact.

Nicholas of Cusa[1]

Inductive reasoning about the afterlife

It was the morning of the world, so everything was fresh and new, looked wet, with strange proportions like a newborn, flowing, springing back to new life. It was the morning of the world, by the ocean, where sunlight reflected on the water was a wide field encrusted with diamonds, and I stared and it polished my eyes. It was the morning of the world, a new beginning. Flowers bloomed and flowers faded, and the blooming was new and the fading was new. Opinions were interesting, and fun to think through. The true meanings of words were easy to decipher, though it was all as intricate as you please.

In the morning of the world, even so-called "inanimate objects" were squirming, flowing, like visual music. I stared into a bush, and it was all lit up inside and cheery, like Santa's workshop. In my treasury are stored up moments. It was the morning of the world, and even an asphalt-paved playground, with its patched, shiny black seams, was oozing intense, dynamic beauty. Light, light, everywhere.

Years have gone by and turned into decades, and every moment brings something new. I am considering again the conceptual coherence of immortality as compared to eternal death – not the immortality of posthumous fame, although I am as vain as anyone, nor the immortality of being absorbed into a greater whole, but the kind of personal, subjective immortality of either continuing to be conscious the way I am conscious now or recovering it whenever I have lost it.

In *God is a Symbol of Something True* I wrote that I didn't believe literally in personal immortality, although I argued that there is a kind of objective immortality of each of our lives in that death can never take away what has already happened. I also declined to identify myself as a Christian, even though I acknowledged my Christian background and expressed the hope that the view I was trying to articulate in that book was consistent with true Christianity. In this book I try to explain why I now believe in subjective as well as objective immortality. Because of this new belief, I'm no longer reluctant to say that my religion is Christianity, for I think of the promise of everlasting life as the hallmark of Christianity.

Does the idea of life after death even make sense? One might expect that those who agree on the answer to this very basic religious/philosophic question would share, by and large, basic world views. However, this doesn't seem to be the case. Among those who would answer No are those who profess not to be bothered by that answer, such as the Epicureans, Hume, and many a modern-day proponent of a naturalistic world view. But there are others who would answer No who see it as an answer that human nature cannot tolerate. Among this second group are those who see this as a cause for despair, like Senancour's Obermann; or for anguish transcended by faith, like Luther, Kierkegaard and Unamuno; or for anguish or nausea transcended by an authentic life of self-assertion in the face of the absurd, like Sartre and Camus.

Similarly, among those who answer Yes, because they believe that it is not difficult to understand how there can be an afterlife and that there is one, there is a divide between those who see this as unquestionably desirable and those who see it as something to worry about or to be overcome. This is important to note because it is often assumed by both nonbelievers and believers of the first type that everyone agrees that surviving death would be desirable. The nonbelievers often use this assumption in a criticism of believers for indulging in wishful thinking, and pride themselves in contrast on being hard-headed realists brave enough to face the truth. For their part, the believers often use the same assumption that everyone would prefer that there be life after death as a reason either to pity the nonbelievers or to be annoyed with them for being unwilling to accept the good that is offered to them. To see that the assumption is false it is only necessary to consider the threat of eternal punishment for sinners in Christianity and Islam, and the goal of escaping the cycle of birth-death-rebirth in Hinduism and Buddhism. To some of those brought up in a culture influenced by any of these traditions, achieving a state of nonbelief in an afterlife might be an easier path to the wish fulfillment of escaping the risk of eternal punishment or the cycle of births and deaths than becoming convinced that one is saved or will return to Brahman or attain Nirvana any time soon. Then, too, as H. H. Price has speculated, there may be many who simply find the thought of death as eternal rest more attractive than the thought of going on and on endlessly.

When we ask if a certain concept or claim makes sense, I think we are asking not only whether it is free of obvious or hidden self-contradiction but also whether it is consistent with other things we think we know to be true.

There is no internal contradiction in supposing that a person can be definitely dead at one time and then at a later time alive again. Those who say that it is contrary to reason to believe in an afterlife in that sense would presumably mean that it is contrary to reasonable expectations based on experience. On the other hand, there is something at the very least paradoxical about the notion of someone being both clearly and unmistakably dead and at the same time alive. The paradox can be resolved either by making a distinction between the person and his or her body or by making one between this world and another one where the person perhaps still has a body of some sort but just not the one that has been buried or cremated here on earth. Then the next question would be whether either of these distinctions is consistent with other things we think we know.

The Hindu sages, Plato, and many people who are neither founders of religion nor famous philosophers believe that a person can shed a body and take on a new one or else exist naked without one as easily as he or she can shed clothing. How many times have I heard or read a student in an introductory philosophy class say, or write, "The body is just a shell," and think to myself and sometimes say, "That isn't a very reassuring comparison, since animals that have shells, like mollusks and turtles, die without them, or else, like hermit crabs, only abandon one when they are very sure the new one is better!" The comparison of the body with a suit of clothes is less alarming, but I can't help thinking that it is a bit far-fetched to compare putting off or putting on a body – something very few people claim to remember ever having done themselves or ever having observed anyone else doing, and something that would generally happen at most twice in a lifetime, at the beginning and at the end – to taking off and putting on clothes, something that we all experience on a daily basis. I don't claim to know that this comparison is inconsistent with what we know. It's just that I don't understand the source of the confidence that this is a clear statement of how things stand regarding life and death – unless, that is, I understand it in terms of a different sort of analogy which gives me more of an imaginative grip on what the experience is supposed to be like. I have in mind the time-honored and yet also perennially neglected analogies between life and dream, death and sleep.

Towards the end of David Hume's posthumously published essay, *Of the Immortality of the Soul*, he asks the following rhetorical question: "By what arguments or analogies can we prove any state of existence, which no one ever saw, and which no way resembles any that ever was seen?"[2] The answer that he expects, and the answer that I too would give is: by none at all. Where Hume takes this to support his conclusion that only Divine revelation could give us any evidence for an afterlife, I take it rather to support the conclusion that we have no reason to believe that death is permanent unconsciousness, since that is a state of existence "which no one ever saw, and which no way resembles any that ever was seen."

I don't deny that we can observe things, such as grains of sand, and stars, that in all likelihood never have been and never will be conscious, although it is possible that parts of these things will be incorporated at some time in the future into beings that are conscious. Nor do I deny that we can observe things like dead animal and human bodies which once were conscious but no longer are. I am thinking about what it is to be conscious or unconscious oneself, not what it is for something else to be conscious or unconscious.

I am conscious and you are conscious, but I have been unconscious relative to how conscious I am now, and I have been more conscious relative to how conscious I am now. Whether or not I have ever been totally without consciousness is not clear to me. What is clear is that I have never been permanently unconscious, since I am conscious now. When Hume writes about the immortality of the soul, I take it that the kind of state of existence he is writing about is the kind that a person might either hope or dread to be in. I note that in that essay he doesn't stand by his famous provocative dictum that "Reason is, and ought only to be, the slave of the passions,"[3] for this is what he says about the doctrine of the immortality of the soul:

> Death is in the end unavoidable; yet the human species could not be preserved, had not nature inspired us with an aversion towards it. All doctrines are to be suspected which are favoured by our passions. And the hopes and fears which give rise to this doctrine, are very obvious.[4]

Hume's argument is that since the only state of existence we have ever known is one of being a living, breathing human organism, we have no way of arguing by way of analogy that after death we are likely to enter into some other, radically different state of existence, such as that of an immortal, disembodied soul, not dependent on air, water, and food. I don't disagree with that, but I do disagree with his (insincere) conclusion, that only Divine revelation could allow us to "ascertain this great and important truth" that we are immortal. What is insincere is not his rejection of an argument for immortality based on natural reasoning but his belief that our immortality is nevertheless a great and important truth that we know through Divine revelation.

Sir Thomas Browne and Joseph Butler both argue by analogy with the metamorphoses of such creatures as silkworms and butterflies that it is understandable how we could be resurrected and utterly transformed as predicted in the Bible. The analogy helps in understanding how such a transformation could preserve biological continuity under radical change, but it doesn't serve as evidence for the prediction, which still depends on revelation. The only kind of experience that can count as evidence for the veridicality of a revelation reported by someone else is either an experience of what is predicted by the revelation, which in the case of Judgment Day hasn't happened yet, or the experience of a similar revelation to oneself. On a psychedelic trip I have experienced a superconscious peak experience so intense that I have no qualms about thinking of it as having died and having been almost instantaneously reborn, and, in a clear sense, states of consciousness induced by 250-500 micrograms of LSD are radically different from non-psychedelic experiences; so I am convinced that such a thing actually happens. As for the parts of Biblical revelation concerning eternal rewards and punishments, these would correspond to good and bad acid trips, making it clear that eternity only seems to last forever.

Of course, my reports will count as evidence for you no more than (and likely less than) the reports of St. John the Divine or other non-psychedelic mystics, since psychedelics are illegal and supposedly passé, unless you are a psychedelic mystic yourself, in which case you have your own direct evidence. However, here I am arguing for the probability of immortality not through any appeal to revelation, psychedelic or otherwise, but only by appealing to inductive reasoning concerning what everyone has and has not experienced.

Hume's premises support a far different conclusion from the one he thinks they do. Since the only state of existence we have ever known has been that of being living, breathing human organisms and since we have no knowledge of being in a state of existence that consists of being permanently unconscious things like grains of sand or like stars, or formerly but no longer conscious things like dead animal or human bodies, we have no way of arguing by analogy that after death we will enter into a state of existence in which we are completely unconscious from then on. Rather, the state of existence we can reasonably expect after death is one similar to the only kind we have known, i.e., as conscious, living, breathing human organisms who need air, water, and food.

Raymond Smullyan puts this more simply by stating that he believes in an afterlife because he can't imagine himself not existing, and he says he thinks that's the real reason, whether consciously or unconsciously, that people believe in an afterlife. He quotes Freud, an avowed unbeliever, in saying that in the unconscious everyone believes he or she is immortal.[5]

This kind of expectation would satisfy Unamuno, who begins his great work *On the Tragic Sense of Life* by saying that he doesn't want to attain immortality by being absorbed like a drop in the infinite Ocean of Being, or by becoming a disembodied spirit. Rather, he wants to be immortal by continuing to have his flesh and blood existence (literally "flesh and bone" in Spanish). It would also satisfy Woody Allen, who said, "I don't want to live on in the hearts and minds of my countrymen. I want to live on in my apartment."

This line of thinking gives rise to an interesting question: Where will I be after I'm dead but continuing to have the same kind of embodied existence I have now?

Where will I be after I'm dead?

One possibility to consider is that I will be here on Earth. When I die, I will leave a dead body behind, but I will have a new one, with no obvious connection or similarity to the previous one, somewhere on this same planet Earth.

Another possibility is that I will have a new body – and in this case it could be one closely resembling my present body – on an Earth-like planet somewhere else in this same galaxy or at least in this same universe.

However, both of those possibilities weaken the analogy between a possible future existence and the kind of existence I have known up till now, each in its own way. In the first one, where I find myself in a different body here on this same Earth, there would most likely be no outwardly detectable memory connections or easily identifiable similarities of bodily or psycho-logical characteristics between me in my old body and me in my new one. Otherwise, we could expect many more convincing cases of identifiable reincarnations than we have. This weakens the analogy because the only state of existence I have known is the one with this body and mind that I take for granted as being mine. Of course, I know of other people having sets of memories, bodily habits, and psychological traits different from my own, but the question isn't whether other people will survive my death. The question is whether I will. And that question gives rise to another one: Given that there are a number of living people, how do I know which one, if any, I am? How do I know who I am? How do you know who you are? I think this is the kind of question like, How do I know what blue looks like? that can only get what sounds like a very uninformative answer: I just do. That is, I know what blue looks like, even though I cannot give an account of how I know it. I could give an account of how I learned to use the word and concept "blue." I could look up a

8

physiological and physical description of what goes on in the environment, including the brain of the percipient when he or she is seeing blue. But those would be answers to different questions and not an answer to the question, How do I or how does anyone know what blue looks like? Similarly, the answer to the question, Given a number of people, how do I know which one, if any, I am? is that I just do know it, without being able to give an account of how I know it.

The various accounts philosophers have proposed, for determining whether or not an experience at a later time and an experience at an earlier time are both experiences of one and the same person, such as Derek Parfit's non-branching psychological continuity or connectedness, purport to tell me only whether two experiences are experiences of one and the same person. If I already know that one of the experiences is an experience of mine, then, supposing the proposed criterion is reliable, it will tell me whether or not the second one is also. But if I don't know whether the first one is an experience of mine or is someone else's experience, I won't know whether the second one is either. Since the criterion doesn't tell me whether any particular experience is mine unless I have already identified at least one other experience as mine without using the criterion, then the criterion is useless as an explanation of how I know any particular experience is mine and not someone else's. I just know it, and since I know it, I also don't need the proposed criterion to determine whether some other experience is also mine and not someone else's. I will just know whether it is or not. So, the problem is not that if I were to find myself with a different set of memories and different physical characteristics, I would have no way of knowing that I was the one so situated. The problem is just that I have no basis in experience for expecting such a thing to happen unless I fall asleep and dream or else wake up from a dream.

The other possibility I mentioned – that I would find myself with a very similar body and psychology but on another planet somewhere else in the universe – weakens the analogy in another way and also points out a new problem with the first possibility. Here the problem is not that I would need to have a body and a psychology different from the one I have now in order to account for the scarcity of obvious evidence for reincarnation here on Earth, since my reincarnation wouldn't be on Earth. The problem has to do with the spatial relations between Earth and the faraway reincarnation planet. How does one get there from here? And this turns out to be equally a problem for the first possibility of reincarnation in a new body on Earth. The closer distance between my dead body and my new body in the case of reincarnation on Earth doesn't really help. Whether it's a thousand light years or a thousand millimeters, by what arguments or analogies are we to prove the transport through physical space of a person from one human body to another, whether or not that new body closely resembles the old one? The process would seem to require being a disembodied soul after all, for at least some period of time, no matter how short.

We have experience of moving through space, and we have experience of noticing physical and psychological changes in ourselves over time. Is that enough to allow us to infer that upon our death we will find ourselves either in a similar body on a different planet or on Earth but with a body and psychology with no evident physical or psychological connections or resemblances with the one we had before? It isn't, because this also would require a period of being a disembodied soul, a state of existence with which we have no acquaintance.

We seem to have reached an impasse. Before suggesting a way to unblock it and reach what I think is a compelling solution, it may be helpful to review the reasoning that has got us to this point.

Accepting Hume's empirical approach to the question whether we have good reason to believe in our own immortality, we agree with him that if a possible future state of existence in no way resembles the past and present states of our existence, then, absent knowledge from some other source such as revelation, we cannot reasonably expect such a future state of existence. We aren't saying it's impossible. We're just saying it is no more probable than many other possibilities we might dream up. We could even say that experience shows that we should expect totally unexpected things to occur from time to time and adopt that also as an inductive principle, but that still doesn't give us a reason to expect any particular unexpected outcome rather than another.

We note that Hume's principle implies that he draws the wrong conclusion when he infers that we can expect to be rendered permanently insensible by death. Neither being like something that has never been conscious and never will be (e.g., a star or a rock) nor being like something that has lost consciousness permanently (e.g., a dead animal or human body) in any way resembles our past or present states of existence. We have no more reason, on Hume's own principle, to expect this than we do to expect the one he is arguing against, that our future state will consist in being a disembodied or reincarnated soul.

Continuing to be conscious or recovering consciousness when we have lost it, and being aware of ourselves as living, breathing human organisms who need air, water and food does resemble our past and present states of existence; but when we consider how to reconcile this with the death of our present bodies, which experience also teaches us to expect, we have to introduce dissimilarities that weaken the analogy. Here on Earth when someone dies, what we observe is a dead body that needs to be disposed of, and, except for a single extraordinary case, we don't observe the reappearance of that same person with a new body closely resembling the old one, nor do we observe, except in a relatively small number of cases, the appearance of someone with a dissimilar body who claims to remember being the dead person and who closely resembles the dead person psychologically. So, if our future state is one of being reincarnated here on Earth, we can expect it to be one that is notably dissimilar to the past and present states of our existence, since we would be unrecognizable to those who knew us before and we might well have no memories at all of our previous lives. Of course, it wouldn't be nearly as dissimilar, to the past and present states of our existence, as being totally and irreversibly unconscious would be (which is probably why Hume said that the theory of Metempsychosis is "the only one philosophy can hearken to"),[6] but it would be dissimilar enough to make us wonder if we have good reason to expect such a future based on our past and present experience.

Could it be that we are reincarnated not on Earth, but on an Earth-like planet somewhere else in the universe? This would explain the scarcity of evidence for reincarnation here on Earth, and it would allow for us to have bodies and minds that resemble those of our Earthly lives as closely as we would wish. But it is a desperate move as an attempt to save inductive probability, for we would have to cross the intervening distance as disembodied spirits, a state of existence which no way resembles our past and present experience.

We have found that there are no inductive reasons for believing in the probability of any of the following states of existence after death: existence as a disembodied spirit, existence as a thing that will forever be unconscious, existence as a reincarnated person here on Earth, existence as a reincarnated person on some other Earth-like planet. Of course, there are other imaginable possibilities, such as existence as a non-human animal, a conscious plant, or a supernatural person; but I think it is clear that the same application of the simple empirical principle, that we have no reason to expect as a probable outcome one that we have never experienced, applies to them as well.

Is there anything that we have experienced that gives us a good reason to expect that we will continue to be living, breathing, conscious human beings dependent on air, water, and food after we die and that is consistent with our observations that living bodies eventually become dead bodies? Yes, there is: our frequent experiences of the transition from being awake to being asleep and dreaming, and from dreaming to waking up.

The dream analogy

Each of us falls asleep and dreams and wakes up every day. If I am awake and I observe someone who is asleep, it is evident that the sleeping person is not conscious of the world around us to the same degree that I am. But I also know that people who are asleep sometimes seem to have richly detailed and emotionally engaging experiences while asleep, and that they sometimes remember these episodes at least temporarily as things they have dreamt. I do this, and I believe others when they tell me they do, too. So, it is quite possible that while from my point of view a sleeping person is unconscious and simply lying there, from his or her point of view he or she is someplace else, engaged in some activity, quite aware of that place and time and those circumstances, and not at all aware of the situation I am observing (or at least not aware of it at a conscious level). It is an easy analogy, then, to surmise that while a dead person appears to be unconscious and just lying there from my point of view, and from the point of view of anyone else who is alive and awake and happens to be there, it is possible that from his or her point of view he or she is someplace else, engaged in some interesting activity, quite aware of that place and those circumstances but not at all aware of what is going on here from my point of view, where he or she has in fact died.

The dream analogy helps me to understand the comparison between the body and a suit of clothes, particularly since I occasionally dream that I find myself exposed in a public place, realizing how wrong I was to have thought that it was perfectly acceptable to go there with no clothes on! If dying is like falling asleep and dreaming, then there is a body that is left behind like discarded clothes (or like the hermit crab's discarded shell). The dead body is no longer occupied by a living person, just as the sleeping body is no longer occupied by a person who is awake.

But on this analogy, the dead person will still have a body with which he or she undergoes various adventures. It just won't be that dead body that other people may see lying there and that gets buried or cremated. A person who is dreaming has a body in the dream. We dream of finding ourselves naked and embarrassed, or running away from a psychopathic killer, or standing in a mountain glade and viewing an incredibly beautiful seascape. The body that is doing these things in the dream is not the same body that other people may see lying in bed asleep doing none of those things, but the person who is dreaming is the person who is sleeping; so in this way the analogy supports the distinction between a person and his or her body that was expressed by the comparison of the body with clothing that can be taken off and put on. Since the dreamer still has a body in the dream, though, the thought that a person can easily exist with no body at all is called into question as having no basis in experience.

If we imagine that dying is a process of casting off the body like taking off a suit of clothes, this raises the question of what corresponds to the naked body that can be clothed in one set of clothes at one time and in different clothes at a different time, and that at a third time may wear no clothes at all. If the body is clothing, what is it that wears the clothes? Not the body, for that has just been discarded. We can answer that it is the soul, the self, the mind, or the spirit, and we have to imagine that this is something without any bodily characteristics, and that each person has one of these as well as having a body. An alternative would be to believe that a person just is a being that always has mental properties and that sometimes also has physical properties. Either way, believing that the body is like clothing that can be cast aside or exchanged for other clothing implies belief in an entity (one for each person) that in itself has no physical properties but that can somehow occupy? inhabit ? take on? a body. Such is not the case with a naked body, a physical thing, becoming covered with clothes, also physical. So, the body is not just like a set of clothes that we wear. So I conclude after all that although I understand how dying could be like falling asleep and dreaming, or possibly even like waking up from a dream, it isn't clear to me how dying could be a process of casting off the body like discarding a set of clothes.

In a dream I have a body. It is not the very same body that an awake person would see lying there asleep, because it could be walking on a narrowing path while that one is just lying there; but it is still undoubtedly my body in the dream, which I usually do not realize is a dream. It is just as dependent on air, water, and food as the body I have when awake. I can be just as anxious of being deprived of the necessities of life in a dream as when awake. I still have to go to the bathroom in some of my dreams, although the dream bathrooms tend to be very unsatisfactory in one way or another, and that wakes me up.

How does my relation to that dream body in that dream world change when I wake up? I no longer believe in it in the same way. I realize that it was only a dream relative to my body now and the world into which I have awakened. It makes sense to me to suppose that dying could be just like that. Here is something that I have experienced on a daily basis, so that if I suppose that when I die I will find the thread of the narrative of this life broken and subsumed like a dream into a new one, I am not engaging in unsupported speculation but rather reasoning inductively on a strong base of experience.

If dying is like waking up from a dream or like falling asleep into a dream, then there is a body that is left behind and a new one that is taken up, but there is no space through which one must travel as a disembodied spirit. There are spatial relations within a dream just as there are within waking experience, but there are no spatial relations between the places in the dream and the places in the world of being awake. If I dreamed last night that I was back again in the old house I haven't lived in for thirteen years, I don't suppose that if someone in my waking life had happened to be there last night, he or she would have seen me there. The vertical cliff side I am desperately managing to cling to in the dream is not perpendicular to the horizontal bed on which I find myself lying when, with relief, I awake. Rather, it has just vanished or turned into my nice, safe bed. I cannot remember any ways in which the body I had in the dream is different from the one I have now – it was just my body – but since one was clinging to the side of a cliff and at the same time the other was lying safely in bed, they were not the same body.

As for temporal relations between the events that seem to take place in a dream and the events of the world of the awake, I can temporally locate a dream event as having occurred on a particular night and even within certain hours of that night if I happened to wake up and notice the time. However, as with spatial relations, there is no strict correspondence between time in the dream and time in the world of the awake. It might have been broad daylight in the dream, and I might have checked my watch to see that it was 1.30 p.m. But then I wake up, and it is the middle of the night. Events in a dream always seem to be happening in the present just as events in waking life do, but I immediately see, when recalling a dream, that the dream events don't fit history as I know it from the standpoint of my waking life. I may dream of people and places that passed out of my life long ago, with all the vividness and sense of presence I have when simply perceiving something at the present moment when I'm fully awake. Or, I may dream of a person or a place or situation or event that bears no relation to my past or present when I wake up but that is reflected in an event in my waking life later that day or even some days afterwards, so that the dream seems somehow prophetic. In terms of objective clock time, however, just as in terms of objective spatial directions and measures, there are no metrics that can be laid across both the world as it is dreamed and the world as it is experienced when awake, yielding uniform results.

It is the very discontinuity that allows us to distinguish between the two and determine when we wake up, that a dream was a dream. When we fall asleep and dream, on the other hand, we ignore the discontinuity and discrepancy between what we seem to be experiencing and what we know from our experiences while awake. We are simply unaware of it, and when we become aware of it and realize we are dreaming, then either we soon forget it once again and go on dreaming or else we wake up.

All I have said so far is that inductive reasoning leads us to expect an afterlife, in that dying will be like either waking up from a dream or falling asleep into a dream. Can we say that it will be more like one of those alternatives than the other? Either way, there will be a discontinuity between this life and the afterlife, whether I am aware of it (waking up) or not (falling asleep); but there will also be some continuities. The spatiotemporal discontinuities in the analogous relations between waking and dreaming show how we can dispense with expecting an answer to the question of where the afterlife takes place in terms of a location in the world as we know it now. Where is that downstairs palace where the rabbit guru confronted me? I can only say that it was in the dream. I can't go find it now that I'm awake. What kind of continuities does the dream analogy lead us to expect? We often dream of people we know and love, including those who are already dead. This gives us reason to hope that we will be reunited with loved ones in the afterlife. (Nietzsche calls this a misunderstanding of the dream, but he doesn't explain what is wrong with it.)[7] Except for some of our most vivid dreams and ones that we have told to others or taken the trouble to record in writing, we usually forget almost all the details of all of our dreams. I have no doubt that I have dreamed countless dreams that I have totally forgotten. (I have also forgotten the details of huge swaths of my waking life.) But if I have totally forgotten them, why don't I conclude that I have no good reason to believe they ever took place or at least that they are of no importance to me now? It is because I remember many times when I have briefly remembered bits and pieces of a dream upon awakening and knew that there was much more to the dream, and now I can't even remember the bits and pieces. Also, there have been times when the mood of the dream remains, and I have the definite feeling that the events of the dream have had a lasting effect upon me. At any rate, it is clear that it was I and no one else who dreamed those things. This shows that the principal continuity that bridges all the gaps between dreaming and waking and waking and dreaming is my own survival. Whether I remember my past moments with crystal clarity, as I sometimes do at least for the moment, or only vaguely or not at all, as long as I am still here – wherever that is (and even if I don't know where that is) – I have survived. I haven't lost my identity.

But back to the question I posed a moment ago, which was whether to expect dying to be more like waking up from a dream or like falling asleep into a dream. Expecting it to be like waking up from a dream goes with a life- and world-denying worldview, as if life as we know it has all been a mere dream and we can only come to know the real truth when we die. In contrast, expecting dying to be like falling asleep and dreaming goes with a life- and world-affirming worldview, but it devalues the afterlife, as if we will lose our ability to think clearly, become confused, dallying with mere fantasies or fleeing terrified from bogies.

Now if we recall that life and the world as we know it includes not only periods like our present state of being awake and consciously thinking, but also every night – and sometimes during the day as well – periods in which we enter that sometimes confusing, sometimes glorious, sometimes frightful state of sleepy dreaming, we see that affirming life and the world implicates us in affirming not only our moments of lucidity but also our moments of being sleepy and confused. It follows that the question of whether we should expect the afterlife to be more like waking from a dream or like falling asleep into one is perhaps not so important as at first it may have seemed. After all, there are degrees of consciousness and wide variations in the qualitative feel of different states of awareness. A state of relaxed daydreaming may be in some ways more enlightening than a state of alert wide-awakeness. And psychedelic experience has taught us that there are states of consciousness which are enlightening to the highest degree without being easily classifiable as either relaxed daydreaming or hair-trigger alertness. They just seem infinitely more fine-grained and intensely colored, both physically and emotionally, than non-psychedelic states of awareness.

Dreaming of waking up

How does our analogy, between dying and either waking up from a dream or falling asleep and dreaming, help us understand how one can die and leave behind a dead body while finding oneself yet still with one's own familiar body? Here the key is to think of dreams in which one faces imminent death – say, a dream in which one is falling from a great height or is being pursued by a wild beast or a murderous human being. There are two possible outcomes: either one somehow overcomes or finesses the threat and goes on dreaming or else one wakes up. The first outcome is analogous to surviving a life-threatening event in one's waking life. The second is analogous to dying. In the dream you find yourself in a life-threatening situation that is rapidly approaching a culmination. The next thing to happen will be what you most fear, and what does happen next? You wake up. You have died to that world of the dream and awakened to resume your life.

When we dream about other people with whom we interact, we believe that they have their own points of view in the dream, just as people in our waking lives have their own points of view. Looking back at the dream, if we consider what other people in the dream would have seen at the moment one wakes up, they would have seen one dying a gruesome death. We know that when people die, the change that will be observed by anyone other than the person who has died is that what was once a living, breathing human being is now a lifeless corpse. So it makes sense to think that, from the point of view of other people in the dream, what happens when from your point of view you have awakened from the dream, is that you have died and are now a lifeless corpse.

This suggests the idea that dying is like waking up from a dream, but there is also a way in which dying is like falling asleep into a dream. From a third-person point of view, sleeping and death resemble each other. Our hope for a dead friend or loved one is that he or she may rest in peace. A sleeping person is unresponsive like a corpse, although to a lesser degree. We may say of a person who is fast asleep that he or she is dead to the world. A person who was asleep often can remember a dream immediately upon awakening, and we know from numerous reports of near-death experiences that people who have regained life after cessation of vital functions have reported experiences of various sorts.

So, instead of thinking that dying is either like waking up from a dream or like falling asleep into a dream, perhaps we should say it is both like waking up and like falling asleep. But how can it be like both of those when they are opposites? A way to answer this question is to think of those times when, to all appearances, one wakes up, only to wake up again later and realize that the first awakening was still a dream. If we take a relativistic view of waking and dreaming, then we can say that being awake is being awake only relative to a remembered experience of not being awake. It may yet be revealed as a state of dreaming relative to a later awakening. There is no absolute state of being awake. One can always wake up again and find that one only dreamed of waking up the first time. But we are equally justified in thinking that the dreamed waking really was a waking up relative to the dream that came before it, as we are in thinking it is a dream relative to the waking up that came after it.

This can lead to the alarming thought that I can never really finally, once and for all, wake up; that I'm trapped in a funhouse, that has ceased to be fun, of mirrors mirroring other mirrors. This is a horror that haunted Poe, and it may be behind the fear of reincarnation in Indian thinking and the goal of liberation from the cycle of birth, death, rebirth. It may also help explain why Christianity and Islam both promise not only an open-ended life everlasting but also, and before that, a final day of judgment, where everything relating to faith, morality, and salvation from everlasting death is sorted out once and for all.

But let's return to our modest inductive reasoning that tells us that we have a strong basis in experience, through our daily transitions from being awake to being asleep and dreaming and from sleeping and dreaming to waking up, such that we can reasonably expect dying to be like waking up from a dream or like falling asleep into a dream. Reflecting on what is shown by the occasional experience of dreaming that one has awakened only to wake up again, we came to a thoroughly relativized way of conceiving of the difference between actually being awake and only dreaming that one is awake, and this led to the worry that maybe one is never really awake, that there is no reality but only an illusory play, spinning out various life situations in an unending and meaningless process.

That worry can be dispelled by further reflection on what experience shows about waking and dreaming. I believe that I am awake right now, and I don't believe it is at all likely that I am going to wake up soon and realize that I only dreamed that I was sitting here writing this. I don't claim to know with certainty that that won't happen. But I do claim I have more reason to believe that it won't than I do to believe that it will. Why is that? It is simply because I remember a great many experiences of waking up from a dream that were not followed by another waking up without first falling asleep again. I remember relatively few occasions on which I woke up and then woke up again to realize that I had just dreamed that I woke up the first time.

Now, as it happens, just last night, a couple of days after having written the above paragraph about the relative rarity of dreaming that one wakes up, I dreamed that I woke up and remembered that I had an appointment with a doctor, and that I was in danger of missing the appointment because I had overslept. I remember trying to check the time and calendar on my phone and being frustrated by finding a sort of gritty, spotty film on the face of it that made it difficult to read. There were many other details that I cannot quite remember now. The upshot was that as my situation seemed to become increasingly desperate, messy, and incoherent, I woke up and realized I had only dreamt that I woke up. I checked the time and the calendar on my phone. The face of it was clear and legible. I had slept only a little later than usual, and I have no appointment with the doctor today. I have since taken care of my usual morning routine, had breakfast, and now I'm writing this. Did I have any reason in the dream, to expect to wake up and find that it was a dream, which I don't have now to expect to wake up and find that this is a dream? Well, yes, in retrospect I did, although I wasn't aware of it until I became aware of it and woke up. That reason was that the details of the dream were becoming increasingly incoherent with what my past experience had been. Of course, this doesn't constitute a proof that I can't wake up again soon and remember that I dreamed I was writing about this, but it suggests that if that is going to happen, what will have to happen first is that some unprecedented and alarming little details begin to pile up or that some unprecedented and alarming big event occurs. As long as that doesn't happen, it is reasonable for me to believe that I am awake, and that I won't wake up again until I have first fallen asleep again.

Besides this modest inductive account of why it is reasonable to believe that what appears to be happening now is not just a dream, I can also reason deductively from the concept of "dream" that if I am dreaming right now, then there must be a waking reality relative to which this is a dream. Even though I am not consciously aware of anything in that reality, I may be in some way dimly aware of it or it may be affecting what I am dreaming. So, the relativistic conception of dreaming and waking does not have the consequence that there is no reality and all is merely a dream. We would be just as justified in saying that there are no mere dreams and all is reality. We are more justified, though, in thinking that sometimes we sleep and dream, and other times we are awake; that these alternate on a fairly regular basis; that, although it is possible that in the future we will sleep and never dream again, or sleep and only dream, and not wake up again, or that we will wake up once and for all and never sleep or dream again, we have no basis in experience that would justify us in expecting any of those possibilities.

Inside and outside

The dream analogy doesn't depend on a distinction between a non-physical entity and a physical one. It only requires a distinction between life as experienced from the inside, from a person's own point of view, and life as observed from the outside, from someone else's point of view. This is the distinction between the concept of a person and the concept of an object. It is necessary to understand this distinction in order to understand the point of ethics. "There is someone in there, just as I am in here." The reason it is morally acceptable to bury a dead body or to cremate it, while it is clearly not morally acceptable to bury someone alive or to burn him or her, is that we recognize that there is no longer someone there in the dead body, while there is someone there in the living body, someone who would hate it just as much as we would to be burned or buried.

It might seem at first that this is a significant difference that counts against the conjecture that dying might be like falling asleep and dreaming or like waking up into a different world relative to which this one is a dream. We think it is all right to bury a dead body. We don't think it is all right to bury the body of someone who is merely sleeping. We need to clarify the analogy then and say that, it is only from the inside, from the first-person point of view, that dying might be like falling asleep and dreaming or like waking up into a world relative to which this one is a dream. Clearly, from the point of view of someone else, there is only a fairly superficial and temporary resemblance between a dead person and a sleeping person. There are easily observable and significant differences such as presence or absence of respiration and circulation of the blood. A dead body undergoes changes that a living body, whether sleeping or awake, does not. So, even though the analogy may be suggested at first by the outward resemblance between sleep and death, it can be sustained and developed only by reflecting on the difference between, on the one hand, what it is like to be awake and aware or to be asleep and dreaming, and on the other, what can be observed about this by someone else. Someone else can be aware that I am aware or that I am sleeping. Someone else may be aware that I am sleeping when I am not aware that I am sleeping but believe instead that I am in church and that someone has laid loose fabric down the main aisle and on the chancel. I will be unaware of that observer of my sleeping body, and he or she will be unaware of what is going on from my point of view. And I may be aware or at least believe myself to be aware of other people in my dream of whom the observer who is awake will be unaware.

Similarly, when I die, it might be that I will be dead from the point of view of anyone who is there to observe my dead body, but alive from my own point of view and from the point of view of other people whom I seem to see around me. This is why it is not relevant to object that we know that consciousness depends on a functioning brain and that dead people don't have functioning brains. They don't have them in this world where they are dead, but they might have them in the afterlife. If dying is like waking up from a dream, then one will find oneself with a brain and body as usual, and it will seem that the brain and body of the previous world from which one awakened was only a dream, relative to that world of the afterlife. If dying is like falling asleep into a dream, then one will find oneself with a brain and body in that dream world, but there will also be a brain and body in a future world to which one will awake again relative to which the remembered brain and body will be only a dream.

* * *

You will have noticed that I have been arguing for a Yes answer to the question of whether it is even conceivable that there could be an afterlife. It seems to me, though, that many of those who say that it is contrary to reason to believe in an afterlife might admit that is conceivable in the sense of bare logical possibility but think inductive reasoning shows that it is highly improbable, and that is what they mean by saying that it is contrary to reason.

I have already argued that the dream analogy shows not only that an afterlife is conceivable while being perhaps wildly improbable, but it also shows that an afterlife is more probable than the alternative. Another argument to the same conclusion begins from the opposite end, and instead of asking whether the idea of an afterlife makes sense, asks whether the idea of eternal death makes sense.

It certainly seems easy enough to imagine that a dead person won't come back to life. After all, in this world, even if we grant that religious believers are correct that there have been cases in which someone has come back to life, and grant that reports of near-death experiences are at least sometimes cases of actual death followed by a return to life, still those cases are comparatively rare and exceptional, compared to all the cases in which people have died and to all outward appearances stayed dead, from ages past right up to the present. Since it is a principle of inductive reasoning to expect well established patterns to continue into the future, it looks as if nothing less than a religious revelation would be required to give us a reason to believe that everyone who has ever died will eventually be raised from the dead. Short of such a revelation, it might be argued, experience shows that at least some and probably most people die and stay dead, and we have no inductively based reason to think they will ever come back.

We need to keep in mind, however, the difference between the inside, first-person point of view on what it is like to be the person having an experience and the outside, third-person point of view of someone else observing a person having an experience. In those cases that have been reported of near-death experiences, if the person in each case had not returned to life and related to others the kinds of experiences he or she had had while, to all outward appearances, dead, no one would have had any reason to suspect any such experiences were occurring. Even in our ordinary lives, each of us has this kind of inside, first-person point of view, such that there are things that we know about that no one else would have any way of knowing about unless we told them. For this reason we have already agreed that it is at least conceivable that someone who is clearly dead, from the point of view of anyone else in this world, might yet be alive and having experiences from his or her own point of view in a world that would be like a dream world in relation to this one, though from the dead person's point of view it would be just "the world," and he or she would be as alive as ever. Our question now is: is it also conceivable from the inside point of view of a person himself or herself, that there will come a time when he or she will cease having any experiences, any feelings, any thoughts at all, from then on, forever?

Notice that the question has to be put in terms of an expectation for the future, because if we put it in the present tense, even in the sense of a timeless present, the answer is simply too obvious, so that it might seem like proving something by verbal chicanery; for then the question would be: is it conceivable for a person to experience having no experience? Or, is it possible to have a first-person perspective on having no first-person perspective? Or, is there something it is like to be nothing? But if we admit that the answer to each of these questions is No, as we should, we should also admit that it is not conceivable from the inside, first-person perspective of a person himself or herself that there will come a time when he or she will cease having any experiences, any feelings, any thoughts, from then on, forever. I'm not denying that there can be gaps in experience, or discontinuities in the narrative thread of one's life, such that a persuasive explanation would be that one has regained consciousness after a period of time during which one was unconscious. What I'm denying is that from a first-person perspective one can imagine a state of being absolutely and irrecoverably unconscious.

There is a clear sense in which a living person can turn into a dead body – before our very eyes – that will never come back to life, as unconscious as any inanimate object, such as a brick or an ice cube. But there is no sense in which a person's own self-awareness can come to a permanent end, even if we observers never again experience any evidence of it. That is why an afterlife is not a bare logical possibility with only a flimsy analogy to support belief in it. The strong inductive case that a dead person will stay dead from the point of view of anyone who is still alive in this world is no evidence at all for the proposition that a person's first-person perspective will go out of existence permanently. Clearly, many kinds of things exhibit no signs of consciousness, and we have no reason to believe that those kinds of things ever have been conscious or to expect that they ever will. But being permanently unconscious oneself is something not only for which there is no evidence but which is not even thinkable. And we each have strong inductive evidence from our daily lives that we can undergo transitions through differing degrees of being relatively conscious, unconscious, and conscious again, without losing our respective identities.

In conclusion, to the question, does the idea of life after death even make sense, my answer is Yes. It makes sense not only in that it is internally self-consistent and therefore logically possible, but also in that it is impossible to think of the alternative of eternal death without falling into self-contradiction, and in that we have a way of understanding what an afterlife would be like based on everyday experiences of falling asleep, dreaming, and waking.

As I remarked in the beginning, however, thinkers can agree

on an answer to this question while disagreeing about whether that answer is something to celebrate or to lament. I said that the idea of eternal death is unthinkable, but it seems thinkable because it easy to imagine the point of view of someone else who goes on living after one has died, from which point of view it will be true that one's dead body will stay dead and will show no more signs of consciousness ever again; and it is easy to overlook the fact that it can only be from one's own point of view that this imagination of another's point of view takes place. No one is a fool for thinking that there is strong inductive evidence that dead bodies stay dead. I can understand how someone can believe for this reason that the idea of an afterlife doesn't make sense and who also thinks that this is a fact that can be accepted with equanimity. But I think they can do this only by not paying attention to the difference between the outside point of view of an observer and the inside point of view on one's own life. There are other thinkers, like Unamuno and the protagonist of Senancour's *Obermann*, who are acutely aware of this difference and who find the thought of eternal death utterly intolerable and a cause for alarm and despair. I think they are wrong to believe that reason tells us that eternal death is our fate. I now believe this thought is emotionally repellent because it is intellectually repellent. Or it is probably more accurate to say that it is an illusion that we can ever really separate our emotional and our intellectual lives. The thought of eternal death literally does not make sense, and the illusion that it is a real possibility is hell.

* * *

Somewhere in Bertrand Russell's writings he tells the story of a chicken who has been fed by the farmer every morning of her life, until one day, when she confidently expects to be fed again, he wrings her neck instead. Am I not like the chicken when I argue that it is reasonable for us to expect a future existence broadly similar to our past and present experience or at least differing from our present experience no more than our present experience differs from our past experience? Well, in one way I am like the chicken. She formed expectations based on experience, and so do I. The reason the joke is on the chicken is because she hadn't observed the farmer wringing the necks of chickens before her, or if she had seen this, she was too stupid to notice and realize that they were chickens just like her whom the farmer had also carefully fed all their lives until the day he killed them. If she had been as intelligent as a human being, she could have foreseen her fate. I'm not denying we're all going to die someday. I'm just arguing that it is unreasonable to expect ever to be permanently unconscious.

At this point someone may be ready to pounce, armed with the objection that my reasoning implies that since the chicken is also a subject of experiences, she can reasonably expect to go on being a subject of experiences even after her neck is wrung. She will just undergo a transition as if falling asleep and dreaming or waking up from a dream and then find herself yet again searching a farmyard for edible grains, cocking her head in her familiar herky jerky manner.

Pounce away, my friend! I do not deny it. We have no reason to believe that any sentient creature has ever experienced what it is like to be a thing that is permanently unconscious like a rock or a star, or a thing that has permanently lost consciousness, like a dead animal or human body. Therefore, we have no reason to believe that any sentient creature will in the future experience what that is like.

Here I expect the objection that of course no one has ever experienced what it is like to be an unconscious thing, simply because one has to be conscious at least to some degree in order to have any experiences at all. But we know very well that there are unconscious things, like rocks and clocks, and we know very well that a thing that is conscious at one time, such as a living animal, can change into a thing that is unconscious from then on, such as the dry, stiff carcass of a possum that was accidentally run over by a car several months ago. And, since experience shows that all living things eventually die, one way or another, every sentient creature, if it knew what we know, would be justified in expecting to become a permanently unconscious thing sooner or later.

My answer is that this is only part of the truth. From my own first-person point of view, I have a body, a living body, and I expect it to someday become a dead body, just as has been the case with all people who have died before me. That dead body will be a thing that has been changed from a living, conscious thing into one that will be unconscious from that point on, as long as it remains an identifiable thing at all. I have no problem imagining my body lying there, lifeless. However, when I am imagining that, I am also imagining that I am seeing it. If I were blind, I might imagine it as if I were touching it or smelling it. And of course to do that I would need eyes, hands, a nose. I'm convinced that I have never seen anything without using my eyes or at least my brain, and I don't know of anyone else who has either. If I am just imagining my dead body lying there, I can also just imagine that I have eyes. Those eyes are just as imaginary as that dead body is, but that isn't what matters. The important point is that I can't imagine my dead body lying there and at the same time imagine my own nonexistence or that I just am that dead body, unless I assume that dead bodies can imagine things. I recognize that this is no problem for anyone else imagining, or actually perceiving someday, that I am dead. They don't simultaneously have to be both dead and yet somehow alive. They can just be alive, and I'll be the dead one. But to imagine my own death, even in my imagination, I must be somehow both dead and alive. There must be a dead body there that I can somehow identify as the one that once was mine and there must also be a living body there that is now mine that is seeing or perceiving through some other sense modality the one that is dead. I suppose I could be a disembodied spirit instead, who is not perceiving my dead body through the senses but instead is just conceiving it. But if I'm just conceiving it, how do I know it actually exists? Well, even supposing that I could somehow be aware of it as a real existing thing without perceiving it through any sense organs, still I would have to exist as a conscious being myself. If I try to imagine a scene where other people are aware of my death, but I'm not aware of anything, where I'm just not there, I may not be there in the scene that I am imagining, as if looking down into a toy world, but that is only because I'm up here hovering above it. In short, I can't imagine myself away. I can't imagine my own nonexistence.

"So what?" I can imagine someone replying. "The fact that you can't imagine something doesn't imply that it is impossible."

I agree. I'm not arguing that it's impossible for me not to exist since I can't imagine not existing. I'm just saying that since I can't imagine it, I can't believe in it. If you want to persuade me that there has ever been or ever will be a time when I don't exist, then you'll need to train me how to imagine it.

It's true that I once believed that it was most likely that death is permanent unconsciousness, and that I simply won't have a point of view once I'm dead; but further reflection has convinced me that I have no basis for thinking that is probable. What I was imagining was this body being permanently unconscious and without a point of view, but then I was also imagining myself as something separate from this body.

It isn't that I have a supersized ego. I don't think there is anything special about me that prevents me from being able to imagine myself away. It is a simple logical point, and I think it applies to everyone. No one has any good reason to believe it is probable that in the future he or she will go out of existence. When we are thinking about other people or other sentient creatures of any sort, we have good reason to believe that they will die, just as we have good reason to believe that we will die; but we also have good reason to believe that from their own first-person points of view, they have life everlasting, just as we do.

Fully mortal, fully immortal

To sum up then, here is the view about the probability or improbability of an afterlife that, as I have argued, we are most justified by experience in holding. There is probably an afterlife, and there was probably a pre-life for everyone who is now alive or ever has been or ever will be; and "everyone" includes not just human beings but all living things. It is reasonable to expect that dying will be like the transition from dreaming to waking or from being awake to falling asleep and dreaming. This analogy implies that after you die you will have a body and that most likely it will be very similar to the body you had in this life. It also implies that the physical world you find yourself in may differ noticeably (at first) from the physical world you previously found yourself in. Because of this, you might be able to do things that would have seemed miraculous in your previous life, or you may be unable to do things you easily accomplished before. Then, either the strangeness will intensify and you will wake up and find that you had been dreaming, or things will settle down quickly into patterns as predictable as ever.

The analogy also implies that you will not be alone. You will encounter acquaintances, friends and family members, without regard to whether they were still living or already dead in your previous life. It implies that you will respond emotionally, from the full range of emotions you have ever felt, in a way that matches the particular situation in which you find yourself. It implies that your psychological, philosophical, artistic, and moral regeneration or degeneration will continue and will be up to you as it has always been.

So far, then, the analogy implies that you are fully immortal. However, it also implies that you are fully mortal, for you are just as vulnerable in a dream as in waking life. If it begins to seem that you are invulnerable, for example that you can magically leap from a great height without getting hurt, then either that episode quickly passes and you forget about it and go on dreaming, as vulnerable to being injured or killed as ever, or you become aware of the strangeness of it and wake up to find yourself as vulnerable as ever.

From a third-person point of view, when a person dies, a conscious, living body becomes a dead, unconscious one. That person has been lost to death, is no longer there to respond. It's as if he or she has gone away, never to return. If you love the person who has died, grief and mourning are inescapable during your waking hours. Eventually, the emotion subsides, but it will never go away completely unless and until you are reunited with the person you loved in your dreams or in the afterlife.

Does the analogy imply without qualification that each of us is immortal? Well, no, it doesn't, because the analogy says that when you wake up from a dream, you have died to the world of that dream. Any fame and fortune or luck in love you had found in that dream slips entirely away, just as much as any hair-raising horrors of it. Of the things of that dream world, an emotional after effect and some more or less vivid scraps of memory remain. In each life you are fully mortal and you want to go on living and enlarging the abundance and joy of it and reducing the injustice and poverty and suffering of it as far as you are able. You fear pain and you fear death, even though it will be the end of any pain caused by the evils of that world, because it will also be the end of any joy attached to the lovable things and people of that world. You leave that world behind, and the analogy tells us that those who loved you will be grieving for you and that even if your name and fame long linger in that world, there will eventually come a time when no one remembers you and not a trace of you remains. But there is something you take with you beyond the grave. Whether or not you or anyone else remembers exactly what happened or even anything at all about what happened, still, it did happen. You lived exactly the life that you lived, in all its painful and joyful details, and nothing – not people's forgetfulness nor the passage of time – can change that ever. It follows that the one thing you take with you always is your spiritual progress. Even though you have forgotten all your past lives, along with – let's face it – most of the details of this life, they have brought you to your current circumstances. Even though the prognosis for this life is inevitable death, and anything you accomplish for the good of this world and these people you love must be done within that limit, you can reasonably look forward to more opportunities to do good in future worlds made up of the same elements but in dramatically or subtly different patterns. And just as you dream of people you know and love, as well as of acquaintances and strangers, you can expect to see them again in the afterlife.

So, you are mortal and you are immortal. Just as dreaming is relative to waking and waking is relative to dreaming, being mortal is relative to being immortal and being immortal is relative to being mortal. You are never absolutely asleep or absolutely awake, and you are never absolutely dead or absolutely alive, but you are always absolutely you. The Socrates of Plato's *Phaedo* was right when he said that the living come from the dead, and the dead come from the living. He was wrong in thinking that in death you don't still have a body, or else he had some kind of knowledge that I don't have.

Afterlife and pre-life

For the same reason that I am unable to imagine never again being conscious after I die, I am unable to imagine never having been conscious before the beginning of this life. There is really no content to the proposition that there will be or was or is a time when I won't, didn't, or don't exist as a subject at all anywhere. For this reason I believe not only that I will have an afterlife but that I had a pre-life also.

There are objections to this view that need to be considered. Here is the first: if I had a pre-life, why do I have no memories of it? And since I have no memories of it, what difference does it make whether I had it or not? Similar questions can be raised about the prospect of an afterlife. The fact that I don't remember my pre-life, supposing I had one, is a good reason to expect that in my afterlife, supposing I will have one, I won't remember having lived this life I am now living. So, there will be no psychological connections between my present self and that future self. I can't form an intention and have any hope that for that reason my future self will carry it out. That future self will have no memories at all of having had any of the experiences I have had, have, or will have in this life. So now it might be argued that there is no content to the proposition that I will be that person in the afterlife. He might as well be somebody else. So, I am no better off than if I were simply mortal and facing eternal death after all.

That would be a depressing conclusion! Let's see if we can't fight it off without sacrificing our intellectual honesty. We can begin by asking the following question: is it true that if I can't remember having had certain experiences that I might as well not have had them? I think a moment's reflection will tell us that the answer to this question is No. A simple example is that there are a great many meals I have eaten of which I now have no memory at all. I have no doubt that I ate them, nevertheless; because I believe I would have some memory of starving at some point in my life if I had actually missed all those meals. So, the fact that I have no memory of the experience of eating those meals doesn't imply that I might as well not have had any such experience in the first place.

If someone were to object that it isn't the experience of eating the meals that matters but only the physical effects of digestion and nutrition, we can consider more overtly psychological effects. Psychologists tell us that people sometimes repress all conscious memory of traumatic events which nevertheless have ongoing effects on the qualities of their life experiences.

Dreams provide another kind of example. Memories of dreams are usually particularly fleeting. Nevertheless, the times when we do remember them seem to tell us that a dream often reflects our ongoing concerns and can impact one's mood and approach well into the following day. I have forgotten almost all of the details of almost all the dreams I have had, but it doesn't follow that I didn't dream them or that they have made no difference to me as I am now.

Similarly, I have no memories that I can identify as memories of experiences that I had before I was born, but neither do I have any memories that I can identify as memories of experiences that I had during the first two years or so after I was born. Sometimes I have quite vivid experiences in which something about my present physical surroundings – often having to do with the way the air feels, the quality of the light and soft noises in the background – seems to be a re-living of a past experience that I cannot identify as being from any particular time in my past, and I feel a sense of opening up into joy and deep contentment. It is possible these could be memories of my very early life. It is even possible they could be memories of a pre-life. I don't know. The main point is that the fact that I have no definitely identifiable memories of a pre-life suggests that in an afterlife I will have no definitely identifiable memories of this life. But it doesn't follow that it doesn't make any difference whether or not I had a pre-life and will have an afterlife. And supposing I did have a pre-life and will have an afterlife, the lack of identifiable psychological connections, such as intentions and memories, between them and my present life, doesn't imply that the person I was in a pre-life, and the person I will be in an afterlife, might as well be someone else.

As Butler pointed out, in criticism of Locke's proposal of "consciousness" as what constitutes personal identity, if I genuinely remember having experienced a particular event, then obviously it was I who experienced it; but this isn't because memory is a criterion that infallibly marks identity but rather because memory presupposes identity. If I didn't really experience the event, then I can only seem to remember it. So, it is possible that I can seem to remember something that didn't actually happen (or at least didn't happen to me), and it is possible that I can fail to remember something that did actually happen to me. There are two reasons why I might fail to remember an event: 1) someone else, and not I, experienced it; 2) I experienced it, but I have forgotten it. This helps to make it clear why the memory criterion of personal identity is useless. Distinguishing between these two reasons presupposes the identity of the person who had the experience.

To return to the dream analogy, if I had a dream that I have completely forgotten, that dream may still result in some lasting effect in my life, even if I remain completely ignorant that that was the source of the change. It could have darkened my mood, for example, with the result that I avoided a social occasion that might have led to an interesting development. Or, a dream that I had forgotten could have manifested itself in my waking life as a sudden insight into a problem that had been bothering me, without my having any memory of the dream itself. The things I do in a dream, the decisions that I make in a dream, could have this kind of carry-over effect in my waking life. So, there could be a continuity of regeneration or corruption of my aesthetic sensibilities and of my moral character from dream to waking life or from waking life to dream.

So, if we imagine that dying is like falling asleep and dreaming, or like waking up from a dream, it doesn't matter, as far as one's survival is concerned, if the dreamer has no memory of his or her life before the dream or if the person who has waked up has no memories of the dream. There could still be important connections between this life and the afterlife. The most important one would be survival. If I wake up from a dream, even if I have no memory of it, the fact remains that I was the one who dreamed it and I am the one who woke up. Similarly, if I fall asleep and dream and have no identifiable memory of that waking world I have left behind, I am the person who was awake and is now asleep.

So, the dream analogy gives us a good reason to believe that the depressing conclusion does not follow. First, it is entirely possible that one did have memories of a pre-life in one's early years that one has now forgotten because back then one had no means of conceptualizing them that would make them identifiable for a long time. Secondly, even if we suppose that there are no memories of a pre-life and will be no memories of this life in an afterlife, it's not true that the person who you will be in an afterlife might as well be someone else. He or she will be you, and it will matter to you that you will be that person, just as it matters to you now that you are the person who you are.

Are other people really there?

Because I have been appealing to the subjective awareness of what it is like to fall asleep and dream or to wake up from a dream, there is another possible objection that we need to deal with before we can enjoy the happy prospect of dismissing the grim illusion of eternal death. It goes like this: my dreams are my dreams, and your dreams are yours, and neither of us knows about the other's unless we tell each other. If dying is like falling asleep and dreaming, then, even if I dream about other people after I die, those others aren't really there. I only dream that they are, and I am isolated and out of any real contact with anybody else. On the other hand, if dying is like waking up into a world relative to which this world was only a dream, then this world is nothing more than my dream, and I am alone, other people again being nothing more than figments of my imagination. So, either I will be utterly alone after I die, or I am already alone and don't know it; and there will never be any way of knowing which of these two alternatives obtains. That in turn implies that even if I am now in the real world or if at some time in the future I will be in a real world inhabited by real people with minds of their own, I have or will have no way of knowing for sure that it is so. If I don't already know it, how could I ever know it?

I believe that I do already know it, because it is clear that when I contrast reality with dreaming, the unreality of the dream is merely relative to the reality of what is known in the waking state. If I dream that I am in a particular set of circumstances involving other people, the person who I am in the dream is no more or less real than the other people in the dream. When I wake up and realize it was a dream, what I realize is that those circumstances now fall under the heading of "dreamed events" and not under the heading of "what is actually happening." There has been a clear break in my awareness of what is going on, such that I now know that what seemed to be happening was only a dream and that what is really happening is that I am now lying in bed awake. However, it has happened to me on more than one occasion that I have experienced the same break in awareness such that I have realized that I had been only dreaming and have been convinced that I was then awake, only for the same thing to occur again, so that I then realized that I had only dreamed that I woke up the first time. There have been other people with whom I have discussed this, who have told me that they have had similar experiences. If you don't remember such an experience ever having occurred to you, I hope you can see that it is at least conceptually possible that it could happen to you, too. Such an experience would be disturbing if we assume that in order for reality to be really real, it must be a final, absolute state of reality that is real not merely relative to the unreality of a remembered dream but such that it would guarantee that one could not possibly wake up again and find that it too was a dream, relative to that subsequent waking reality. However, if we assume instead that our conception of reality, by which we believe a waking state to be real in comparison to a dream, is a conception of a relative, not absolute, reality, then we need not worry that there is no way we can know for sure that we are really awake. If I wake up and remember a dream, I can be sure that I am really awake in relation to that dream, even if I soon wake up again and realize that I only dreamed I woke up the first time. One and the same state of awareness can be a waking state relative to a remembered dream and a dream relative to a subsequent waking state.

Suppose I tell you that I had a dream about you. You wouldn't have known it unless I told you or unless I told someone else who told you. But as you appeared in the dream, you were as aware of what was going on as I was. Now that I am awake it is clear that you and I did not both have that same dream. It was my dream and not yours. (I don't mean to imply that it is logically impossible that two people could both dream of the same events, each from his or her own point of view. I'm just supposing we are considering the usual case.) This is the reason for the worry that if dying is like falling asleep and dreaming, or like waking up from a dream, then all I can know is my own dream, and everyone else is only a character I am dreaming up. You as you appeared in my dream did not really have a mind of your own. The dream, including a seemingly independent you, was entirely the product of my mind. At least that is what we both might assume, now that I am awake and telling you about the dream. This all depends on our reasoning, now that I am awake and telling you my dream, that because I was aware of what I was dreaming and you weren't, I had a mind of my own in the dream and you didn't; or, in other words, that solipsism is true in a dream. But if we know that solipsism is false just by analyzing the concepts of "I," "mine," and "self," then it is false in a dream as well as in waking life.

Solipsism, the view that the only person who exists is the thinker of these very thoughts, is false because the concept of who I am and what is mine can only be understood in a context in which there is at least one other person – you, or he or she, or they – who can join me so that not only I am but we are. If I try to think a thought such as "Only I exist," or "I can't know that anything exists outside my mind," the concepts of "I" and "my" lose their normal meaning, and it isn't clear what other meaning they could have. If there is only one self, it is no more I in particular than it is you or anyone else. And all of us together are not that one self either, because it is one and we are more than one. So, the self who is no one in particular would not be what we call a self. So, it is false that there is only one self.

But there may be a true solipsism as well as a false one. If we think of what it is about each subjective point of view that makes it a subjective point of view – that is, caring, striving, and enjoying – or if we think about a potential mutual acknowledgment between every point of view and every other; we may approach the concept of "I" for whom solipsism is true, where "Only I exist" thought by me not only does not contradict but equals "Only I exist" thought by you. This true solipsism would be the same thing as Christian love, which is God.

The fact that I know about my dream about you, and you don't know about it until I tell you, is no different in kind from the fact that now that we are both awake, there is always something that I know but that you don't, and something that you know but that I don't. I can even know things about you that you don't know. For example, I might notice that the tone of your voice changes whenever you talk about a certain person, while you may not have been aware of that at all until I pointed it out. I know how the world appears to me, and you know how the world appears to you. I can tell you about how the world appears to me, and then you can know something about it too, although it will never be to the full, rich extent that I experience it directly. But then you have your own full, rich experience. You can tell me about how the world appears to you, but I can never experience your experiencing of it. It certainly doesn't follow that you don't have a mind of your own or that I don't. And in my dream, likewise, you could have told me about your perspective, and I wouldn't have known until you told me.

Finally, let's consider a theological line of objection to my claim that the same reasoning that convinces me I will have an afterlife also tells me that I had a pre-life. Someone might object that only God exists necessarily, that the existence of any creature, including me, is contingent, and so my conclusions are tantamount to claiming that I am equal to God, or that together we all are, since none of us can conceive of himself or herself as not existing.

Here is why I am not claiming to be God. The choices I make are an indispensable part of a complete account of what kind of person I am, but one choice that is not mine to make is which person, out of all the persons there are, I am. That is just a given fact, and it doesn't make sense to me to think of it as given by an impersonal nature. That is a good reason to believe in a personal God.

* * *

Suppose I dream of a Platonist, a scientist, and an idealist having a conversation.

Platonist: The things we seem to know through our senses are real only to the extent that they remind us of things in the world of Forms that transcends this world.

Scientist: What is real is what our best scientific theories tell us is real, and science assumes there is a reality that is independent of our knowing minds but that we can come to know through empirical observation and scientific theorizing.

Idealist: The existence of a sensible object just consists in its being perceived. This table here is real because we can all four of us see it, touch it, hear the sound it makes if I thump it – thwack! But there is no "real table" in a world independent of our minds which is causing us to have those sensations. The table just is the collection of all those sensations or potential sensations that a perceiving mind could have of it.

When I wake up and realize that I only dreamed that these three people were saying these things, what light does the realization that it was only a dream shed on the question of the truth of what each of them asserted?

What the Platonist said was true in that there is a world that transcends the world of that dream he was in, namely, this world to which I have now awakened. The reality of the things and people in the dream derives from, or reflects, or is identifiable by way of resemblance to, the things and people of this world to which I have awakened.

What the scientist said was true of this world to which I have wakened. However, I may with good reason suspect that if he had expounded any particular scientific theory that explained the events in the dream, it might well have differed from the science of the world into which I have wakened, since I may recall dreams in which I was capable of things that are physically impossible when I am awake, such as flying effortlessly with no machine or apparatus, or jumping from a great height without being harmed.

What the idealist said about the table was true. It was real for me the dreamer and for the other characters in my dream just as long as I was dreaming of it. But now that I have awakened, I have no reason to believe that that table must still exist somewhere, on the grounds that common sense tells us that things like tables and chairs and sticks and stones have an existence independent of the minds that perceive them. It might be better to say that the dreamed table does still exist in the only sense in which it ever really existed relative to this world to which I have awakened: as a table in a dream. And the same thing will be true of the idealist himself, along with the Platonist and the scientist. But what about me? I alone exist not only as the observer of the conversation in the dream but also as the awakened rememberer of the dream. I have no reason to assume that the Platonist, the scientist, and the idealist each also awakened at the same moment somewhere else in this world to which I have awakened.

But again, this line of thinking seems to lead to solipsism. Other people come and go. Of course, some of them have a much more enduring place in my life than others, but I myself am the only one who is always there – even if this world would turn out to be a dream from which I have awakened.

Let's suppose for a moment that that is true, that is, that I have woken up and am only remembering that I was dreaming that I was writing this book. I wouldn't find it lying around anywhere or stored in a computer. In fact, I would be shocked if I did see it, or if I came across it while browsing online or at a library or a bookstore, should any of those things exist in the hypothetical waking world we are imagining. It is true that in addition to those three I have identified as a Platonist, a scientist, and an idealist, I might have also dreamed about people I know from my waking life; but they would have no memory of what happened in my dream. That seems to be a reason to believe that a person, other than me, whom I know in my waking life, is not strictly speaking the same person I may remember having dreamed of, so in that way Platonism seems true about people as well as about other things. I identify the person in a dream in reference to the person in my waking life. That person now that I am awake has no memory of the events in my dream, while I do remember those events, at least for a short while.

But here is why solipsism doesn't follow. If that lack of psychological continuity, between the dreamed person and the person with whom I identify the dreamed person now that I am awake, is a reason to discredit the strict identity of the dreamed person with the one in my waking life, I will have equally strong reason to discredit the strict identity of me now that I am awake with myself in the dream. The lack of psychological continuity is not that I have no memory of being the person in the dream, for we are supposing that I do. The psychological break is from the other direction. As I was in the dream, I had no anticipations or intentions, concerning the person that is now awake and remembering all of that as a dream.

A possible objection would be to claim that an important difference between my relation to my dream and your relation to my dream, supposing I tell you my dream about you, is that I can learn more about myself by reflecting on the dream I remember, while my dream about you doesn't reveal anything to you about yourself, other than the fact that I dreamed about you. But since the roles we play in each other's lives form an essential part of who each of us is, this objection is unconvincing. You learn something about how you "come across" to me, about the role you played as an archetype reflected in my dream imagery. And similarly, I can learn something about myself if you tell me about how I appeared to you in a dream.

Then if part of what makes you you is how you appear to me, and part of what makes me me is how I appear to you; it is plausible that the person who appeared in my dream, and whom I identified as you, actually was you, or at least an aspect of you, and similarly for me and the person you dreamed of and identified as me. In other words, a full account of a person's identity includes not only that person's objective circumstances and subjective experiences but also the subjective experiences of others in which he or she plays a role.

And yet there is still something unanalyzable about personal identity, in that a subject of experience always eludes capture in any objective description. Suppose I am given a thorough description of a person's physical appearance and location, and of his or her psychological characteristics, including facts about what this person remembers, desires, loves and hates and the roles he or she plays in the lives of others and other notable biographical information. I would know, if the description was complete enough, whether or not I was the person being described. If I were suffering from amnesia, the description of my present immediate surroundings and physical appearance would need to be more detailed than if I had normal powers of recollection, but unless I had only instantaneous perceptions completely isolated from each other – in which case I wouldn't be able to understand the description or anything else – I would still be able to know whether or not I was the person being described. But this isn't because personal identity, or the ongoing existence of a person, can be analyzed by virtue of a bodily criterion or a psychological criterion or a combination bodily/psychological criterion. It is because it is simply a given fact that I have the particular subjective point of view that I have, for if I had a different one, I would realize a different answer to the question of whether or not I was the person being described.

Suppose you were the person being described. Then if I had your subjective point of view, I would realize that I was the person being described. But this is just to say that if I were you, I'd be you, a tautology we already know without any analysis. What makes me me is that I experience the world from my own particular subjective point of view, and what makes you you is that you experience the world from your own particular subjective point of view. We can talk about what each of us experiences from our respective points of view, and the fact that we can do this and understand each other is the fact that there is an objective world independent of any point of view in particular, though dependent on being experienced from some point of view or other. But if we subtract the givenness of my subjective point of view for me and yours for you, from the way the world is objectively, no analysis, no matter how detailed, of what constitutes the continued existence of a person, would yield the fact that I am the particular person who I am and you are the particular person who you are.

Without this extra information for each person, of which person, out of all the actual persons, he or she is, the objective description of what constitutes various continuing lives would be like a map of an unknown territory without a "You are here" starting point. With this information, i.e., one's own subjective perspective on the world, the answer to the philosophical/religious question that matters: Have I survived? – will be given. For any given person in the future, I will either experience the world from that person's first-person perspective or I won't. If I do, then any other connections that will exist between me now and me then are irrelevant for the purpose of answering the question about personal identity. I may hope that I will then remember my present life, but whether I remember it or not has nothing to do with whether or not I will have survived. Again, the dream analogy helps to make this clear. The fact that I have totally forgotten a dream doesn't imply that I didn't have the dream or that I didn't wake up.

Someone (e.g., Locke, Parfit) might object that surviving with no memory of my past self is just as bad as not surviving at all. For example, if I was Socrates but have no consciousness at all of ever having been Socrates, this is no different from having been someone else – Hitler, say – with no memory at all of ever having been he. On the dream analogy, this would be like saying that if I had had a beautiful dream full of marvelous insights into the ultimate nature of reality but have totally forgotten the dream and its insights, this would be no different in its practical effects from having had a horrible nightmare full of confusion and rage, which I have also totally forgotten.

In reply, I would say first of all that it is doubtful that the lack of a cause and effect relation of which anyone is consciously aware implies that there would be no practical effects. There could be effects on my unconscious mind that only psycho-analysis could discover. However, the objection could then be modified to take this into account by saying that unless there is some kind of effect that could at least theoretically be detected, there would be no difference between my having been Socrates and my having been Hitler, or between the dream and the nightmare. In other words, such a bare survival with no psycho-logical connections from past to future would be worthless.

But this objection is only partly right. What is right about it is that if we contemplate a kind of existence in which there is absolutely no conscious connection between past, present, and future ever, this would be like no kind of human existence at all. What is wrong about it is that that is not the kind of existence I am contemplating when I say I believe that whether or not I will be a person in the future doesn't depend on whether or not that person in the future can remember any of what I can now remember or experience or expect. Nor does it depend on any other criterion such as bodily continuity between me now and that future person. It will only depend on whether or not I will then be experiencing the world from the perspective of that person.

In my experience I have always had memories of a personal past and expectations, fears, and hopes of a personal future. That is the kind of existence I hope to continue to have in the future, since, as I said, an existence as a series of disconnected moments, each with no past and no future wouldn't be like any kind of human existence I know. It doesn't follow that there is nothing to prefer between not surviving at all and surviving as a person who has a past and a future but who has totally forgotten about the experiences of my present life, not only consciously but in any way that could be recalled under hypnosis or psycho-analysis. When I wake up, I have a past and a future, and whether or not I remember a dream, I am the person who was asleep and is now awake. Similarly, I could die and lose consciousness and then later regain consciousness as if waking up from a dream in a future life with its own memories and expectations for the future, even if I then had no memories of this life.

There is one way in which a future life will always be connected with a past life, assuming it is given that they are both lives of the same person, me, for example. Whether or not I or anyone else knows it, it will be true that I had those experiences, made those decisions, and acted in those ways. So, the aesthetic and moral value or disvalue to which I contribute in this life will have the continuity of being either a case of growth or decay from my contributions in the previous life.

More on what difference it makes

I don't want to die, and this isn't just a momentary lack of desire, as when I decline a glass of water. I can imagine that I find myself in circumstances where I would want to die in order to escape physical or emotional or philosophical pain, but I have never actually found myself in such circumstances – unless I unconsciously wanted to die in my dreams because I somehow sensed that there was something monstrously unreal about what was going on and that is why I woke up. However, although I argued in *God is a Symbol of Something True* that simple mortality might be preferable to the alternatives I described there, I still shrink from the thought of death as the final, once-and-for-all end of my subjective awareness. I would prefer that dying be simply a discontinuity or disruption followed by a new narrative thread that is taken up, or rather, as it would more likely seem, resumed, as the dream analogy implies. Death in that other, ultimately final sense, eternal death, seems to sit there waiting for us, mocking us, belittling us, not caring one whit how long or well we live, ready to snuff us out at last with brutal indifference. But why does this seem so horrible? If I really get snuffed out with brutal indifference, I will no longer feel any brutal indifference or any gentle caring. It won't be like anything at all. It will just be a blank. Is that right?

I spoke of philosophical pain. What is that? It is the inability to make any sense out of what is happening. At first, it seemed that death might be a way of escaping it, the way that death seems to be a way of escaping physical or emotional pain. I've read that the most dangerous sign of a suicidal tendency in someone is not just the thought of doing it, since as soon as a young person learns that some people have actually killed themselves, he or she might entertain the thought that this is at least an abstract possibility for him or her as well. The dangerous sign is when the thought of suicide begins to seem comforting, as an escape from physical or emotional pain. But I don't think it can ever seem comforting as an escape from philosophical pain, for the thought of death as simply a great blank, the end of one's subjective awareness from then on forever, is itself a source of philosophical pain. It is incomprehensible, uncanny. It doesn't make sense. That is why it seems so horrible. It is repugnant to the intellect.

Once again, I anticipate the objection that the fact that something is incomprehensible doesn't prove that it can't happen. No, but if I can't comprehend it then I have no reason to believe in it, because I don't even know what it is.

So, my first answer to the question, "What difference does it make to think of dying as being most probably instead like the transitions between waking and dreaming?" is that it dispels that shadow that seemed at times to lurk around every corner, the doom of eternal death; living while believing that you have life everlasting is a much more lighthearted but not frivolous affair.

It isn't frivolous, because the second answer to the question, "What difference does it make?" is that it shows the supreme importance of ethical and aesthetic values.

Now when I say that I don't believe in eternal death and believe instead that dying is like the transition from dreaming to waking or waking to dreaming, I can imagine someone challenging me as follows: "OK, then, suicide must not be so awful, and it could be a way to test your sincerity. If you are willing to kill yourself – not in order to escape unbearable pain but rather to demonstrate your sincere confidence in the strength of your inductive reasoning to the conclusion that there is an afterlife and that there was a pre-life, then I will be impressed by your confidence (or dismayed by your fanaticism), even if I still believe you were wrong. I don't want you to kill yourself. But if you are not willing to kill yourself, then that must be because you're still more afraid of eternal death than you are confident of an afterlife."

I said you are never absolutely asleep or absolutely awake and never absolutely dead or absolutely alive. My reasoning doesn't tell me that for all I know I may just as well be dreaming right now as awake, nor that I may just as well be dead as alive. I believe that I am awake and alive, and I don't want to fall asleep and dream just now, because I'm not tired and I want to keep writing right now; and I don't want to fall down and die, because I'm not tired of living. When I do get tired, it will be fine to fall asleep and dream and later to wake up refreshed. I hope that when it comes time to die, it will also be all right in that it will be like resting from the burdens of this life by falling asleep and dreaming and later waking up refreshed into a new life. But the analogy only says that dying is like the transition from being awake to falling asleep and dreaming or like waking up from a dream. It doesn't say it just is falling asleep or waking up. The difference is that if I anticipate falling asleep and dreaming for a while and then later waking up, I expect to resume this life upon awakening, with the only change being whatever changes the dream has wrought upon me plus whatever changes in my outward circumstances that may have occurred during those hours. Those people of my waking life I leave behind when I fall asleep will see a sleeping, living body if they are still awake and look at me, and when I wake up they will still be there. When I anticipate dying, I expect that from my point of view in the afterlife, things will be going on in what will seem to be a more or less normal way, including the presence of people I know and who will know me there as someone who is just as alive as they are. However, I also expect that those I left behind in my previous life will see a dead body lying there, that they will have no reason to expect that after a few hours I will wake up and rejoin them, and that instead they will need to be making funeral arrangements.

So, yes, the effect of the analogy is to make one lighthearted in comparison to the at best disguised or temporarily forgotten heavy burden of belief in or worry about eternal death, but it doesn't render one incapable of telling the difference between going to sleep for a few hours and dying. It removes the burden of being haunted by the specter of eternal death, but it doesn't lessen one's interest in one's present life and its duties. Jesus said, "My yoke is easy; my burden is light." He didn't say, "There is no yoke; there is no burden."

The desire to go on living is not a whim or some strange quirk unique to me. I recognize it in all living things, and it is the source of the supreme ethical principle that Albert Schweitzer called reverence for life. After all, this will to live is the basis the skeptic uses to accuse the believer in everlasting life of wishful thinking. In order to make the accusation the skeptic thinks, "I, too, would like to believe in everlasting life, but I am willing to face the fact that there is overwhelming evidence for the belief that when the body dies, so does the soul." One such philosopher, David Gunn, even goes so far as to say that it is the death of the soul that causes the death of the body.[8]

We need to distinguish between the will to live and the will to believe in an afterlife, since the skeptic presumably has the former but lacks the latter. Or perhaps we should say that the skeptic has no desire to give up the will to live but does desire to give up the will to believe in an afterlife, assuming he or she ever had it. Once we make this distinction, it is clear that the skeptic and the believer are on the same ground. The skeptic has his or her reasons for desiring to give up belief in an afterlife, or for not adopting such a belief if he or she never had it. The believer has his or her reasons for desiring to acquire or maintain belief in everlasting life. The question then is who has the better reasons, not who is indulging in wishful believing.

Speaking personally, I believed I had good reasons not to believe in personal immortality when I wrote *God is a Symbol of Something True*, and I tried to explain those reasons, but I didn't think this implied that I should also give up the will to live. I don't know of any skeptic about personal immortality who does think that. On the contrary, those who deny the world and life, believing we should mortify the will to live this life, tend to be believers in personal immortality, like the early Christians, Hindus, and Buddhists.

The sweet spot is to believe in everlasting life without mortifying the natural will to live this life. If I have a greater will to live now than when I didn't believe in an afterlife – and I'm not sure I do – it isn't because I have a greater will to live than I did before that I now believe in an afterlife. The causality, if it is there at all, runs the other way. It would be because that heavy burden of doom has been lifted from me that I have a greater will to live (if it really is any greater).

This brings us back to the burden that remains, and why it is an easy one. The burden is the duty to act in a way that is consistent with reverence for life in all its forms, based on the recognition of the will to live in every living thing – the very same will to live that I experience directly in myself. It is a light yoke and an easy burden, not because it is undemanding or easily fulfilled, which it isn't, but because it is liberating and joyful to realize that there are no genuinely moral duties that are imposed from without. The only true moral ideals are those that you recognize from within. As soon as you recognize an ideal, such as reverence for life, you realize also how far short your efforts to live up to it fall. Nevertheless, every time you act consistently with your ideal, in even the smallest way, you atone for the times you have fallen short, and you have a fresh beginning.

On this question, I regard myself as a follower of Albert Schweitzer, who notes that we are surrounded by living things, each one doing things that help it maintain its life and to flourish in its own way. Yet these beings often come into conflict with each other. They compete with and destroy each other. The maintenance of the life of one depends on the death of another which does not willingly sacrifice itself. Nature, even our own nature, is inconsistent with our ethical ideals. We yearn for a peaceable kingdom in which living beings care for each other as much as they care for themselves, so that life is not divided against itself. Schweitzer teaches that although it is impossible to live and affirm life without accidentally or deliberately sacrificing the lives of some living creatures, every time we act in such a way as to preserve and enhance the life and well-being of any living creature, even the smallest and seemingly most insignificant, when this doesn't require sacrificing the life or well-being of another, we thereby affirm the world and life in a way that is consistent with our own will to live, and the more we do this, the more we make amends for the times when we have acted thoughtlessly.

You are surrounded by other living beings, and it is within your power to help or to harm them in the simplest, most down-to-earth ways, or simply not to care what happens to them. From within, I recognize that ethics oblige me to act with mercy and not cruelty or indifference. I should treat those within my power the way I hope to be treated by anyone who has me within his or her power.

But nature has you within its power and you cannot realistically hope for it to be merciful.

True, but it would also be wrong to think of it as cruel or indifferent. Such moral descriptions simply don't apply to nature, even human nature. You cannot derive egoism from nature any more than you can altruism. Natural law ethics doesn't work. The only way to know what natural law is, is through experience and inductive reasoning. But all that that tells us is that sometimes people are kind, sometimes they are cruel, and sometimes they are neutral. We can't appeal to human nature to explain why a particular person at a particular time chooses to be kind or to be cruel or indifferent. We explain a person's actions as a result of his or her individual moral character, and at the same time our only evidence for a person's moral character is his or her actions. You are what you do.

Suppose someone says, "Yes, I want to go on living, and I can recognize that other living beings also want to go on living, but my will to live is the will for me to live above all, and some other being's will to live is the will for him, her, or it to go on living above all. Any particular individual's will to live is not the same thing as a will that every or even any other living being go on living. So, how can you derive an ethical obligation from the recognition that other living beings have a will to live just as you do?"

The answer is that it isn't a matter of deriving an ethical obligation from something else. It is matter of taking upon oneself an ethical obligation. To the question, "Why be moral?" the answer is, "So you won't be divided against yourself and so that you will have a richer and fuller life." The you who wants to go on living is the living you, is life itself manifesting itself as you. It is the same life itself that manifests itself also as all the other countless living things. This isn't a matter of overcoming the ego. The poor ego has had enough bashing from philosophers like Alan Watts and Huston Smith, both of whom I otherwise admire very much. If you denigrate your ego, you denigrate everyone's ego. It is morally bad to be a selfish person, that is, someone who tends to look out strictly for his or her own interests without regard to what anyone else wants. However, this doesn't imply that it is wrong to have interests of one's own, or that it is a good thing to suppress them.

When you recognize that other living beings want to go on flourishing in full life just as you do, you may still choose to sacrifice the lives of some living things in order to preserve the lives of others. Schweitzer himself willingly prescribed antibiotics to kill the microbes that cause sleeping sickness in order to save the lives of his patients. Yet he insisted that is wrong to think that some lives are more valuable than others.

One might wonder, then, on what basis he decided that it was his duty to save the lives of his patients at the expense of the lives of the microbes that caused their disease. Don't we think it would be morally wrong to let a fellow human being die for the sole reason that saving his or her life requires killing whole colonies of microbes, each of whose life is every bit as valuable to itself as our friend's is to himself or herself? Yes, and I think Schweitzer would agree. But how does his ethical principle of reverence for life explain this?

I confess that it isn't completely clear to me how Schweitzer would answer this question, but I would hazard a guess that it would be along the following lines. Whether or not it is what he would say, it is what I would say. "Reverence for life" is a phrase that expresses a way of viewing the world as life itself as lived from within – breathing, pulsing, growing, squirming, reaching, flowing, melting, grasping. One walks up a suburban sidewalk, and all is footsteps, bird calls, traffic sounds, breezes, the smells of flowers and a wood fire. Trees are alive, birds are alive, grass is alive. I am alive. This is something precious, of absolute value. But I must eat in order to stay alive and this involves taking the lives of other living things in order to sustain my own life. I believe that it is worse to kill other people and eat them for food than to kill subhuman animals for the same purpose; worse to kill a mammal than a fish, and worse to kill a fish than a plant. But that isn't because some lives are more valuable in themselves than others are. It is because there are other valuable things within life besides life itself, and human beings are more capable of creating and appreciating those things than subhuman animals, and mammals more than fish, and fish more than plants or microbes, even though every single living thing is valuable in itself, and none more than any other.

It is conceivable that there could be living beings more capable than we are of creating and appreciating valuable things, and that we could be a food source for them. If we were the only possible food source for them, then we could expect them to believe that it is morally permissible for them to kill and eat us, and we wouldn't be able to object on moral grounds when they managed to catch us. However, we would be justified in condemning them morally if they gorged themselves or captured and killed us in unnecessarily cruel ways or for sport. Furthermore, if we suppose that these superior beings discovered that they could subsist as well or even better on a diet of plant based foods, then if they persisted in eating us out of habit or stubbornness and claimed to be morally justified in doing so because of their superiority, they would be wrong.

Henry Sidgwick, the great Victorian era British moral philosopher, argued that the supreme good is not life but desirable consciousness, and that we value life only because it is a necessary condition for desirable consciousness. If we value life only inasmuch as it is a necessary condition for desirable consciousness, then life that doesn't involve consciousness would have no intrinsic value and neither would consciousness that was not desirable. Thus a state in which there were living things none of which were conscious would not be preferable to one in which there was no life at all. And a state in which there were conscious beings who were conscious of nothing but misery might even be worse than one with no life at all. We only tend to think a state of no life at all would be the worst because in our experience life does support consciousness and enough joy to outweigh the misery it sometimes also brings.

I used to believe that Sidgwick was right about this, but I no longer do. How are we to conceive of a state of no life at all? It is supposed to be no worse than a state with life but no conscious life and preferable to a state with life and consciousness but only miserable consciousness. Well, I agree that a state with living things that lacked even the slightest glimmer of consciousness and with no potential for ever developing consciousness would be no better than a state with no life at all. But what would it mean to say that there is life but absolutely no consciousness and no potential for ever developing consciousness? What would prevent it from ever developing consciousness? Perhaps its environment is destroyed before there is enough time for it to develop consciousness. But it wouldn't follow that it didn't have the potential for developing consciousness, and would have done so if it hadn't met an early demise.

Here I have the same problem I have with imagining my own non-existence or total and permanent unconsciousness, for I am trying to imagine a state in which I don't exist or in which I am never conscious to imagine anything. It's the old uncanny, intellectually and emotionally repugnant doom of eternal death. It isn't just a state of relative unconsciousness out of which consciousness might return. I have no problem imagining that, but I do have a problem in imagining a state of total and final unconsciousness, whether I am trying to suppose it is accompanied by unconscious life or not.

Similarly, when I try to imagine a state with life and consciousness and unrelieved misery, and ask myself whether eternal death wouldn't be preferable, I run into the same problem of being unable to imagine either eternal death or unrelieved and utterly hopeless misery – eternal death for the reasons already given and unrelieved misery because I've never experienced that either in a way that in retrospect would make me glad that I had exchanged it for eternal death.

I've never experienced unrelieved and utterly hopeless misery. I have suffered in a way that verged on being unbearable, and I don't think I'm special in that way. I imagine you have, too. But although it seemed I just couldn't stand it a minute longer, it never actually reached the point of being unbearable and hopeless, because of course I did bear it and until it went away I went on hoping it would. And my hope was eventually realized. I know that some people kill themselves because they lose hope that anything else could relieve their suffering. I don't condemn them for doing it. It is heartbreaking that some people reach this point. However, I do think they are wrong, because in my own experience there has always been something other than killing myself that did relieve my suffering, even when it seemed like nothing could. Conditions changed. The old chestnut, "This too shall pass" was verified again.

* * *

It has happened a few times in those hours of vulnerability when I'm tired and trying to get to sleep, my defenses are exhausted and I'm at the mercy of my imagination doing its worst before it does its best, that I have imagined in the most vivid, concrete way what it would be like to be a condemned prisoner spending his last hour, his mind struggling with the concept of his own imminent annihilation – except it's not he, not somebody else. I'm the one to die. It's a feeling of sheer panic. Convinced that any physical struggle with the guards, any attempt to escape, would be hopeless, it is now a purely mental struggle, a spiritual struggle. In less than an hour now – and the time is ticking relentlessly away – the merciless machinery of the state will cause my heart to stop beating. I will stop breathing. I will lose consciousness and have no more experiences forever and ever.

Or, I'm at the mercy of a hardened criminal or a fanatical terrorist, or I just have a heart attack and drop dead, as my Daddy did one day without warning, a day that still brings tears to my eyes sometimes when I am alone.

So there now, haven't I just imagined it after all? Everything just comes to an end, for me, though not for everybody else. There is just a blank, nothing, as when you turn off a television – only it never comes back on ever again, and it isn't just a television; it's the whole world. Well, the whole world doesn't go out of existence for other people, but just for me. Would it be worse if everybody died all at once – killed, say, by a giant asteroid smashing into the Earth or some even more universal catastrophe killing every bit of life everywhere in the entire universe? At first, I am inclined to say Yes. It seems there would be some consolation in the fact that life will go on and that it's just my life that's going to come to an end now. But after all, all living things die, so it's just a matter of timing. The world will go on, a few people will be aware that I have died, and some may even miss me; but most will be unaware that I ever lived, and even those closest to me will go on with their lives, as will everyone else – until their time comes, too. Sooner or later we each flicker out like a candle, and die our own deaths, sucked into the void, never to breathe, talk, eat, have sex, or even just walk across a room again. And it's going to happen to me in just a few minutes! I don't want to die, but they're going to kill me anyway. There is nothing I can do about it. I can't reason with them. They have no choice in the matter, or at least don't think they do. And anyone who does have a choice, and realizes it, has chosen to do this. I can only reason with myself. Is there any way I can make sense out of this, make it seem all right, or at least give up the struggle? Well, sure, I'll give up the struggle – when I quit breathing!

Now have I succeeded in imagining my own non-existence? How can the thought of my life being taken from me against my will be so horrible unless I am succeeding in imagining my own non-existence? What I am succeeding in imagining is being faced with imminent death. I don't want to die, at least not now, and it may be that I will never want to die. So, the thought of being killed or of dying of a heart attack or cancer is horrible to me. But what makes it horrible is thinking that it is equivalent to the cutting off of any future.

I have always had a future. One of the things that make death seem so tragic is the way it brutally disrupts a person's plans for the future. Other people die and still one's own death is off in the indefinite future – until it isn't, until it comes, and then not only is it no longer in the future, nothing is. But is that right?

People plan for their death by planning what is to be done with their property when they die, and, to the extent that they are able, by providing for the loved ones they leave behind. It seems that the only way to plan for an afterlife, by people who believe that they will have one, is to live the right kind of life in this life now. However, appeals to the notions of divine reward and punishment in an afterlife, as a motivation to virtue, have always struck me as childish and crass. Now that I am convinced there is an afterlife by my inability to conceive of my own non-existence, I need some positive conception of what an afterlife might be like. That way, I can make sense of having plans for a future life in a way that is not childish or crass.

How an afterlife might make sense

So, here is a recapitulation of what I've been saying about the probability of an afterlife. Hindus, Buddhists, Pythagoras, and Plato got it partly right with the doctrine of reincarnation or metempsychosis; but the goal is not for the individual ego to be dissolved into Brahman or to be liberated from the cycle of death and rebirth or from the prison or tomb of the body. That just gets me back to my inability to imagine my own non-existence, or else to the unattractive prospect of existing as a disembodied soul with no new experiences.

Religious Taoism and Unamuno the Catholic existentialist get it partly right with their insistence that nothing less than real physical immortality will do, but religious Taoism makes immortality seem too much like an achievement only attained by a few through esoteric means, and Unamuno makes it seem like something that doesn't make sense but should just be accepted on faith. It isn't that I think nothing should be accepted on faith. It's just that I think we at least have to understand what it is we are accepting on faith. Otherwise, our professions of faith might be mere empty words.

Judaism, Christianity, and Islam get it right that each individual person goes on existing and is of ultimate worth, and consequently stress the importance of justice, mercy, and especially in Christianity, love. Where does the "but" come in here? Well, I am a Christian but a Taoist sort of Christian. The Taoist part indicates my squeamishness at the thought that God wants to be worshipped and will punish those who refuse. The Christianity I endorse is not hostile to Judaism or to Islam, and gives a different "twist" on the conception of the afterlife.

I'm guessing that the afterlife will be, as in Hinduism and Buddhism, like a series of incarnations. It won't be like a permanent heaven or hell. It won't be all that much different from this life. There will be joy, sorrow, grief, ecstasy, love, hate, day-to-day concerns of obtaining one's daily bread. There will be some heavenly periods, some hellish ones, and a lot that are neither heavenly nor hellish. The transition from this life to the next one will be like the transition from dreaming to waking, or from waking to dreaming, or from one dream into another. There will be periods of super-consciousness in which one is fully awake to the heart-breaking beauty of the world and human life, and there will be periods of dull and troubled lack of appreciation. There will be restful sleep and troubled sleep.

One will still be mortal and will have to face death again, but it won't seem like "again" because there is enough discontinuity between one life and the next that all the details of the previous life will be forgotten, and only vague feelings of recognition will remain. But there will also be a certain amount of continuity between one life and the next, just as there is between our waking lives and our dreams. We can rationally hope we will be reunited with our loved ones, just as people we love, whether dead or alive, appear in our dreams.

The point of supreme importance is that you don't have to worry about being sucked away into nothingness. Yes, candles are lit and go out. Mountains rise and are eroded. Stars begin to burn and burn out. Living organisms spring up and die away. But you – what makes you you and not somebody else – has always been here and always will be. You have always had a past. You will always have a future.

You are limited within this lifetime to things you can accomplish within this lifetime, and it will be that way in your future lifetimes also. It is important to set goals and to accomplish them, but when those are accomplished, there are new ones. There are beginnings and there are endings, but there was no beginning to the beginnings and endings, and there will be no end. Genesis happens every time. If you want to accomplish something in this life, then you have to do it before you die; but if you don't, it is still possible you may do it in a future life. Thus there is the urgency of mortality but backed by the relaxed confidence of immortality.

Return again and again to the dream analogy. In a dream you have a body and confront physical limitations as well as psychological challenges. When you wake up, it's as if you have died to that dream world. You are no longer in it. But you still have a body. Is it the same body? In a way it is, and in a way it isn't. The physical laws that obtain in a dream are often quite different from those in this our common waking world. The spatiotemporal locations in the dream have no spatiotemporal relations to the spacetime of this our common waking world. You may have dreamed last night that you were back again in your old house or at a place where you worked years ago, but it doesn't follow that if someone had gone to your old house or your previous place of employment last night, they would have seen you there, or that you would have dreamed of them as present there. You can tell us where your old house is; but if we ask where the events of your dream took place, the only answer is: in the dream.

This solves the population problem for the doctrine of reincarnation. Each lifetime gets its own spatiotemporal world, and the worlds are related by resemblances and differences, but not by spatiotemporal location, except in the sense of past, present, and future.

This brings up another longstanding objection to a doctrine of reincarnation. Some people claim to remember previous lives, but most people don't. If I have no memory of a previous life, what difference does it make whether I had it or not? And similarly, if I have a future life but have no memory at all of this one, in what meaningful sense will I, as I am now, continue to exist in that future life?

The answer, again, is to appeal to the dream analogy. I assume that, like me, you have forgotten all the details about almost all of your dreams; but it doesn't follow that it wasn't you who had those dreams, and it doesn't follow that they have no meaning for your waking life, although it does follow that you are not conscious of the ways in which those dreams signify something about the way you are now.

Now someone might object that we at least remember some of the details of some of our dreams – usually the most recent or the most dramatic or meaningful ones – whereas most of us don't remember anything about any of our past lives, assuming we have them, and it is possible that none of us do, if the few who do make such claims are frauds or are deluded. In reply to this objection I admit that the analogy is imperfect in this way but still maintain that it is helpful in understanding how the concept of an afterlife (and a pre-life) could make sense. The fundamental reason for believing in immortality is the inconceivability of one's own non-existence. Try and see for yourself if you can imagine your own non-existence.

I am trying to think of how to conceive of an afterlife and a pre-life in a way that is consistent with what we have all experienced in this our life together.

The dream analogy also provides a solution to the worry that everlasting life could turn out to be boring, trivial, or meaningless. In reading the *Iliad* it struck me that only the mortals had a capacity for nobility, for heroism, *because* they could and did die. For the immortal gods, nothing was really at stake. No matter what happened, they would go on playing their childish games, as spectators of their toys the mortals. Similarly, when reading John Hick's description of what the world would be like if all possibility of evil were removed, I found myself objecting to Hick's defense of theism by asking, "But isn't that what Heaven is supposed to be like?" That is, in a world with no possibility of suffering, of death, of evil; the moral virtues, such as charity, heroic self-sacrifice, self-control, are unnecessary. If no suffering is possible, what is the point of compassion? Also, if one goes on living, forever and ever, wouldn't there come a time when one had lived through every possible experience over and over again, so that the old dream of immortality would come to seem like a cruel joke? Then one might indeed see the goal to be liberation from the cycle of death and rebirth, and yearn for one's life to be snuffed out like a candle in complete darkness once and for all.

The solution is forgetfulness. Waking up from a dream is like dying to the world of that dream, but one is reborn into the waking world. There can be continuity from dream to waking life, in terms of one's moral and artistic progress, but there is a narrative discontinuity between the chain of events in the dream and the chain of events in waking life, and most often one quickly forgets all but a few details of the dream. There seemed to be a natural progression that led to my finding myself in that strange situation, but now when I try to recall it, it is very elusive. A few interesting details stand out, along with a vivid feeling of the emotional tone evoked by the dreamed circumstances. There may be a lesson learned that remains also. But the lessons can only be applied in the context of the exigencies of one's daily life in the waking world that soon take over.

The solution is that we really do die, and we really are reborn, so that each lifetime is a new one, and in it there are horizons on both sides. We can't remember in any definitely identifiable detail a past life or what it was like to be born, and our dying is always off in the future, until it looms near, and then we can tell other people what that's like, i.e., what it's like to be near death, but then when death comes, it's too late to tell anybody what *that's* like.

It is a doctrine of Christianity that Jesus Christ is both fully human and fully divine. How can that be? Well, you are supposed to wonder about that. We have the story of His prayer that "this cup be taken from me" and "yet not what I want, but what you want." (Mark 14:36) We have his outcry on the cross,

"My God, my God, why hast thou forsaken me?" (Matthew 27:46) But we also have the story of the Transfiguration and His saying "the Father and I are one."(John 10:30) I'm not going to say that, just like Jesus, we are fully human and fully divine, because at the very least I think we can confidently say that if you and I are fully divine, we aren't fully conscious of it. The Hindus say we are fully divine, but we have forgotten and are dreaming the dream of maya. The goal is to wake up and realize it. But then we aren't fully human *and* fully divine, because it is an illusion that we are separate from Brahman. But I don't think that's right either. What I would say instead is that we are fully mortal and fully immortal, and I think that is consistent with being a Christian.

The joy of welcoming a new person into the world when a woman gives birth, the grief of losing a loved one to death, the passage of time over a lifetime, the gaining of wisdom through experience – these are as real as anything can be. I reject any philosophy or religion that counsels us to view them as illusory. The worry was that if we truly had everlasting life, life would become trivial, boring, or meaningless like the lives of the Olympian gods. The answer is that on the analogy with dreaming and waking, there are beginnings and endings; but also you have past life extending unendingly into the past and you have future life extending unendingly into the future. You have it now. The way it will be is the way it is. If your present life is not trivial, boring or meaningless to you, there is no reason to fear that the afterlife will be either.

Transcendence and immanence

We must integrate the conception of God as immanent with the conception of Him as transcendent. The dream analogy tells us that there is always an outside to our inside that is presently inaccessible to us. But what happens here and now will have symbolic meaning for that future there and then. When I wake up, there is a sense in which the dream is less real than the reality into which I awake. But that I dreamed the dream that I dreamed is no less a part of my history than anything else I do or that happens to me, whether I remember it or not. There is nothing unreal about the emotion evoked by the dream. If I pay attention to what I remember of the dream, I may learn something about myself. The reality of the waking world that is out there and inaccessible to me while I am dreaming corresponds to the transcendent Heaven to come and the transcendent God. The reality of the dream, which is accessible, working itself out, corresponds to the Kingdom of Heaven on Earth and the immanent God. They are both always there. Admittedly, this is vague, but I'm afraid it's the best I can do, at least for now.

The dream analogy indicates that most likely we won't find ourselves in the afterlife in a permanently Heavenly or permanently Hellish condition. Rather, we can expect relief if our life has become relatively hellish, or a slight disappointment if our life has become relatively heavenly, and otherwise nothing more than a brief recognition of where we are, quickly fading into taking our new life for granted. Doesn't Christianity tell us something different?

Yes, the official creeds tell us, with some scriptural support, that we will be raised from the dead on Judgment Day, unless it happens during our lifetimes, and that from then on, those who have done good will have everlasting joy while those who have done evil will be in everlasting torment. The everlasting joy of

Heaven, where everyone loves each other and there is no more sin and strife, is a goal worthy of our hope and faith. But there is a passage in the Gospel of Luke in which Jesus says, "The kingdom of God is not coming with things that can be observed; nor will they say, 'Look, here it is! Or "There it is!' For, in fact, the kingdom of God is among you." (Luke 17:20-21) In the non-canonical Gospel of Thomas, there is a very similar passage that is even more explicit: "It will not come by waiting for it. It will not be a matter of saying 'here it is' or 'there it is'. Rather, the kingdom of the father is spread out upon the earth, and men do not see it."[9]

We have both the transcendent permanent goal and the immanent, though transitory realization of the goal. There are moments in life that are heavenly, when like wise gods, we have no enemies and are full of serene joy, love, and pity. True, they don't last, but part of what is understood then is that it doesn't matter that they don't last. It is enough that they have happened, even if we go on to forget about them. But we don't completely forget about them.

Now, what about the clause that says that those who have done evil will be everlastingly conscious of being eaten by worms and will never cease feeling the pain of being burned? Just as there are heavenly moments in life, there are also hellish ones of physical and emotional pain. If we are to believe that the transitory nature of the heavenly moments doesn't matter because they are always in a sense there, aren't we obliged to believe the same about the hellish ones? Due to accidents, diseases, natural disasters, and – even worse – the actions of fellow human beings, people suffer, sometimes horribly. If we go the route of dismissing suffering and evil as illusions, we are likely to end up with one of those world-denying views that disrespect the immanent heavenly moments of this life also. Let's not do that.

Punishments, rewards, tests

I can see three options on the question of the traditional doctrine of Judgment Day resulting in eternal punishment for unrepentant evildoers. We can simply accept it, we can simply reject it, or we can accept an interpretation of what it might mean as if we had dreamed it, while rejecting a simple, literal interpretation of it. You won't need three guesses to pick which of these alternatives I'm going to recommend.

Let us suppose a man has murdered two people who did not deserve to be killed and has then turned the gun on himself. Given what I've recommended above about viewing the afterlife on the analogy with dreaming and waking, each of these three people – the two victims and the suicide/killer – will find himself or herself suddenly in a different situation, as if waking up from a nightmare and carrying on a familiar life. There would be hope of eventually reaching that transcendent Heaven where there is nothing but joy forever and ever, and in the meantime there would be the usual mixture of joys and sorrows they had become accustomed to in the past of their present lives, with the transitory moments of immanent heaven.

It is natural to feel that this is all well and good for the two victims, but considering the grief over their loss on the part of their loved ones who remain behind in this life and considering the preferences of the victims to go on living their lives without being murdered, it is entirely unfair that the killer also finds himself in a similar situation. Assuming there are no extenuating circumstances that would excuse him, he is morally responsible for taking the lives of his victims against their will, and he deserves to be punished.

On the traditional view, if he was unrepentant at the time he killed himself (and even if he repented of the murders and that is why he killed himself, he would have had to repent of the suicide itself at the last split second in order to get off the hook), he *will* be punished – endlessly. There is no hope for him, ever. Now it is too late for him to repent.

While it seemed unfair for him not to be punished at all, it also seems unfair for him to be punished endlessly. Infinite punishment for a finite crime is surely unduly harsh. There are those who defend it by saying that the crime is not really finite, because the lack of repentance, the disrespect for the gift of life given by God, being a sin against an infinite being, deserves infinite punishment. But why does the extent of the crime and the appropriate punishment depend more on the status of the victim than it does on the status of the perpetrator? And does it make sense to think of God both as punisher and as victim? It doesn't as far as I can see.

Here is another problem. If we are interested in the temporal rationale for punishing evildoing, the point is to prevent the evildoer from doing more evil and to deter others from following his or her bad example. That gives us a reason to impose punishment, whether the evildoer repents or not. If he or she does sincerely repent, we take that into account and impose a lesser penalty on the grounds that he or she is less likely to repeat the crime and is a less bad example for others. But if we are interested in the moral, spiritual, or religious rationale for punishment, then the punishment in question has nothing to do with the kinds of penalties that are imposed from outside, for the purpose of preventing or deterring further evildoing. For punishment to have any moral, spiritual, or religious value, the evildoer must willingly take it upon himself or herself.

A solution is to believe that punishments for one's evil deeds, just like rewards for the good ones, are internal and automatic, known and felt directly and immediately, as well as in the long run, in the way one perceives the world as a friendly or unfriendly place. The truth then is not that punishment is eternal or endless but only that you can't escape your guilt by forgetting about it, by falling asleep, by waking up, or by dying. All you can do is to accept that God forgives you, to suffer gladly whatever suffering you must undergo in consequence of your actions, and to do good and sin no more.

For example, suppose you wake up from a dream in which you were doing something so awful that you would be ashamed to tell anyone you had even dreamed it. Even though during the dream you seemed to have a rationale for doing it, you are now shocked and disgusted by the memory of it. Your punishment is that you realize that even after it fades from conscious memory it will still be a fact that you dreamed it.

To say that rewards and punishments are automatic sounds a lot like the doctrine of karma. What needs to be added is the doctrine of salvation by grace, which avoids the determinism that is implicit in the doctrine of karma. If you are convinced that every good deed is automatically rewarded, and every bad deed automatically punished, by the law of karma; then why don't you always do only good deeds and never do any bad deeds? Suppose you encounter someone who is suffering and you have the means to relieve his suffering. According to the doctrine of karma, he is suffering as a direct and automatic result of something he has done, whether in this life or a past one. You decide to help him, because otherwise you would be building up some bad karma of your own. But is that really a free decision of yours, or is it itself just the working out of karma? The fact that he is now relieved of his suffering would be fully explained in terms of karma as due to some good deed he has performed either in this life or in some previous one. But since this good karma of his resulted in his receiving your act of kindness, and it is the automatic result of the ironclad moral law of karma, then it appears that you did not do it of your free choice after all. You make a free choice when two or more equally possible alternatives are open to you. But even though it may have seemed to you that you could have chosen not to help him and that you

chose to do so, that unchosen alternative was not a real possibility, because his good karma automatically ruled it out. In that
case, how can you earn any merit for it? And if instead you had
refrained from helping him, then that also must have been
because his karma was too bad for him to deserve the good
fortune of receiving your help, so your failure to help him is
determined by his past bad karma. So, your refraining from
helping would not have been a free choice of yours either and
thus not something for which you deserve demerit.

If truly spiritual reward and punishment is internal and
automatic, manifested in how one views the world, and cannot be
imposed from without; the fact that someone has been hurt or
helped by someone or something else cannot be any evidence as
to whether the person is being spiritually punished or rewarded.

The Christian doctrine of salvation by grace says that we can't
save ourselves by our own efforts; rather it is given freely
through God's grace. If I do a good deed in order to be saved, this
shows that I don't realize that I am already saved, that I haven't
accepted the gift that God has freely given. The relation between
doing good and being saved is the other way around. If I have
freely accepted that I am saved, then I am more likely to do good
deeds because they spring forth naturally from a confident and
joyful heart. But still, I am a sinner, so I say "more likely to do"
rather than "will do," because it doesn't seem possible constantly
to maintain that realization of being saved; that possibility gets
put off to the hoped for goal of being in that transcendent Heaven
in the future. But there is also the goal of realizing again and
again, transitory though it may be, the immanent heaven – "Thy
Kingdom come, Thy will be done, *on Earth* as it is in Heaven,"
when it seems superfluous and ungrateful to hope for any later
Heaven. The upshot is that I am free to do good or not, so I am
morally responsible and get rewarded or punished automatically,
not by any outwardly discernible state of joy or misery but rather
by my own ability or inability to interpret my pleasant experi-

ences and my painful ones in a way that contributes to spiritual progress.

Each of us suffers at times and at others feels joy. Suppose you're suffering. One possibility is that you are being punished for your sins. Another is that your faith is being tested. A third possibility is that there is no spiritual significance to your suffering. It is just something that has happened and it can't be helped. How could you know which of these interpretations is the best? It will depend on the particular situation. Suppose the suffering takes the form of a splitting headache, and you had too much to drink the night before. In such a case it makes sense to think of it as punishment for your sin. You did the crime; you're now doing the time; you can resolve to remember this the next time you are tempted to overindulge. Suppose, though, that the headache has just come out of the blue with no clear connection to anything you have done. In such a case, the punishment inter- pretation wouldn't be helpful. Which would then be better: to think of it as a test of your faith or as something that had just happened with no spiritual significance? If the headache is relatively minor, if aspirin or some other pain reliever helps and you eventually realize the pain has gone, then it might seem overblown to interpret the suffering you had to endure as a test of your faith. At any rate, it would be an easy test. But suppose the headache intensifies and turns into the worst headache you have ever had. Eventually, someone takes you to the emergency room, and it turns out you have had a stroke. In such a case, the choice between a spiritual or a non-spiritual interpretation is more momentous and indicative of your philosophical and religious stance. On the spiritual side, the question of whether or not this might be punishment for your sins might arise again, depending on whether or not you have a very guilty conscience. Supposing you don't, there is a choice between interpreting this as a test of your faith or as simply a misfortune with no spiritual significance.

The skeptic might ask, "Who is punishing you or testing you?" A religious answer would be that God or the law of karma is doing the punishing, but if this is your deepest self, then you are punishing yourself. Could the stroke or, in a different case, the cancer be the result of your unconscious self punishing your conscious self? And could the same kind of answer be given on the interpretation that you are being, not punished, but rather tested? Tested by God, or by your deepest self?

To interpret physical or emotional pain as punishment could be right if you have good reasons for feeling guilt, i.e., if you really have done something you shouldn't have, and if you can be redeemed by the pain. However, if you have internalized some powerful figure's erroneous judgment, interpreting your pain as punishment is to harm yourself wrongly.

We don't have the same problem with the interpretation of physical or emotional pain as a test of faith. Tested by whom? By God or by your deepest self. Martin Buber would say, by the eternal You. Where it can be damaging to interpret pain as punishment, resulting in nothing more than further, unnecessary and unjustified suffering, I can't think of any way it could be harmful to interpret pain as a test of your faith.

A possible objection would be that if the pain doesn't eventually go away, if, let's say, it just gets steadily worse because it is due to a terminal illness; then viewing it as a test of your faith could naturally turn into the punishment interpretation after all. If you had faith that all would somehow turn out for the best, that you could recover from mistakes and temporary setbacks, then in the case of pain until death you might not be able to help feeling that you had failed the test and that your suffering was punishment for your failure.

One way to answer this objection is to admit that it is possible that one will fail the test of faith, whether in that imagined scenario or in some other, which would also be a case where it would at least seem that the worst possible outcome had occurred. Even Jesus hoped that his faith would not be tested and advised his followers to pray that theirs wouldn't be either. But this presupposes that it is possible that one's faith will be tested, and a real test is not something with a guaranteed positive outcome.

Another way of dealing with the problem of interpreting pain until death as proof that you can't always recover from your mistakes, and that things don't always turn out for the best, is to be convinced of your immortality by reflecting on your inability to conceive of yourself as non-existent. Yes, you really are mortal. You will have a death date, as you had a birth date. There are projects that you can only complete in this life, and if they don't get done, they don't get done. But you are also immortal. You can't really go out of existence. Moral and spiritual progress (or regress) and aesthetic enlightenment (or degradation) carry over from one life to the next, just as they do from your dreams into your waking life and from your waking life into your dreams. So, the fact that only death relieved your pain would be no indication that you had failed the test of faith and were accordingly being punished.

In fact you passed the test of faith, and it's happening again and again and again, in a creative outburst of vibrant colors, fascinatingly complicated shapes, unbelievably rich textures, flavors, aromas, heavenly music, courage, tenderness, love. And living your daily life, with its struggles and successes, is the way to express your relief.

Psychedelics

In the morning of the world, there was a poster on a wall, blue and gold, a mandala that appeared to be breathing and stretching around the curves of its design with a barely tolerable, achingly intense beauty. The words, "Sat Chit Ananda" were printed at the bottom. "What does that mean?" I asked my friend, whose mom was a member of the Self Realization Fellowship.

"Being Awareness Bliss," he replied.

Elegant commentary.

It was the morning of the world, but it was also the middle of night, and the Devil appeared. "I don't believe in the Devil," I said to myself, "but this must be the kind of experience people have who do." Shortly after that, I became aware of my heart beating violently, rapidly. Sheer panic terror. I couldn't go on that way. And yet I did, pacing back and forth, holding on during the wee hours of the morning until daybreak and things were better. But then It would return, only not quite as bad as before, then subside, return – but again not as bad, then subside, until that pattern faded into the background. Being with people close to me helped so much.

Still, it was the morning of the world, and everything was new. It was the Day of Creation. For a long time I was an atheist. But how can an atheist think, "This is the Day of Creation"? I was an atheist because I didn't believe in a supernatural Person who was like a stern but loving Father. It didn't make sense to me to think He was out there somewhere, or in here. Well, maybe in here, but that wasn't supposed to be good enough. I was an atheist, but I was religious. I had religious experiences. I was open to there being truth in the Bible, but I couldn't stand the idea of being bribed and bullied to believe.

I discovered philosophy. No disapproval of non-belief there, rather a demand that beliefs be justified. That way you can discover that you don't really believe what you thought you believed, that you believe something else after all, that is more consistent with other things you still believe.

After many years I have changed my mind about death probably being permanent unconsciousness, and now I'm a kind of Psychedelic Christian, I think. Although I haven't taken LSD or any other major psychedelic in decades and may never again, the psychedelic experiences I had in the past stand out as some of the most memorable experiences of my life and serve as a standard for understanding what life is all about. I'm a Christian because I believe in and aspire to live up to the great Christian themes of forgiveness, loving kindness, and life everlasting for each and every individual.

I am well aware of reasons people might have for being skeptical about both the psychedelic and the Christian sides of this worldview, and that, as life is complicated, simply stating a creed doesn't get us very far. So, first I want to address the drug issue and then the sins of Christianity issue.

One motive for taking an illegal drug is to seek a pleasurable, temporary rest from dealing with one's problems. Thus we have the term "recreational drug." Some people frown on this motive and abhor the very idea of using a drug for recreation. Some of them are even consistent about this and abstain from the legal drug, alcohol. Others think there is a significant difference between the recreational use of alcohol and the recreational use of any of the illegal drugs. Of course, the fact that one is legal and the other isn't is itself a significant difference, but in order to justify that difference, one would need to point to some other significant difference. The ratio of lethal to effective dose for heroin is half of what it is for alcohol; that is, the risk of dying from an accidental overdose of heroin is twice the risk of doing so with alcohol. That could be a justification for keeping heroin illegal and alcohol legal. However, there are other illegal drugs, notably marijuana and LSD, for which the risk of dying from an accidental overdose is practically nil and estimated to be 100 times less likely than with alcohol. Even cocaine has a better lethal to effective ratio than alcohol by a factor of one-and-half to one. So we can't justify in that way the status quo, where alcohol is legal and those other drugs aren't.

Another factor to consider is how addictive a drug is. If one becomes addicted to a drug, so that stopping it leads to withdrawal symptoms and using it becomes habitual and obsessive, then it can no longer be considered carefree and recreational. Here again, though, it is hard on these grounds to justify the status quo in which alcohol is legal and LSD, for example, is illegal. Alcohol may be somewhat less addictive than heroin and perhaps cocaine, but it is still highly addictive, especially for some individuals; and, despite the fact that alcohol use is free of the extra problems caused by being illegal, the misery caused by addiction to it is well known. LSD, by contrast, is not addictive at all in the sense of causing withdrawal symptoms.

Marijuana is probably the safest drug of all in terms of the risk of death through accidental (or even deliberate!) overdose. But I don't think it is quite as non-addictive or anti-addictive even, as LSD. I have no doubt that some people, at least for a while, get into the bad habit of thinking they need to enhance every experience by ingesting marijuana beforehand in a way that results in their lives being actually less enhanced than they would be with more moderate use. Still, I can see no good case for making marijuana illegal and alcohol legal. The argument that marijuana is a so-called "gateway drug," in that people who use it tend to move on to using worse illegal drugs and so it should be banned, is faulty on two grounds. First, the premise is false if it means all or even most people who use marijuana go on to use worse drugs. Secondly, if it means that, if not a majority at least a sizable number of them do, it is true but then if one thinks the premise, so interpreted, supports the conclusion that marijuana should be banned, one would be stuck with an argument that proves too much. Surely, a sizable number of alcohol users go on to use marijuana and then to use worse drugs, so alcohol should be banned. Surely, a sizable number of aspirin users go on to use alcohol, then marijuana, then worse drugs, so aspirin should be banned. Surely, a sizable number of milk drinkers...

I've said that LSD is non-addictive and even anti-addictive. By "anti-addictive," I mean "tending to be used less and less frequently over time." And LSD doesn't fit the model of "recreational drug" anyway, not because it is something worse than that, but because it is something better than that.

We know that there is a danger of accidental overdose and the bad consequences of addiction in regard to many drugs, both legal and illegal. We also know that there is a danger of accidental death from engaging in dangerous sports and other pursuits, such as mountain climbing, skiing, race-car driving, skydiving, flying private planes, etc. We also know that some people become addicted to the thrills of such pursuits, increasing the risk of injury or death. It is also clear that many people have very differing attitudes to the two types of case, and that because of this, laws have been passed against the production, sale, possession, or use of many kinds of drugs, while the production, sale, and possession or use of the equipment involved in the dangerous non-drug activities as well as the activities themselves are completely legal and socially acceptable.

How are we to account for these differing attitudes? I think it has to do with the distinction between recklessness and courage and the different way that it applies or fails to apply in the two types of case. Someone who has courage is willing to do something in the full knowledge that it is dangerous to his or her health and even survival, if doing so is necessary to protect someone or something of such a value that it merits that risk. We believe that there are people and ways of life that deserve to be defended even if it requires such a risk. We admire people who take such risks for such a purpose. Recklessness is the willingness to take risks without regard to such purposes. We think it is a shame if someone is severely injured or killed by being reckless. We think it heroic, the very opposite of shameful, if someone is severely injured or killed by being courageous.

Whether out of courage or recklessness, there can be a thrill involved in facing and surviving a dangerous situation. Some people are more attracted than others by that thrill, and it is reasonable to think that in a situation that calls for courage, a person who enjoys danger would be more likely to stand up to fear than someone who habitually leans more towards caution than thrill seeking. This might explain why many people admire those who pursue dangerous activities like mountain climbing, auto racing, sky diving, etc., even when these activities serve no purpose of protecting someone or something that deserves to be protected and in fact involve risk to something that deserves to be protected, namely, the health and life of the person pursuing the dangerous activity. There is the feeling that these are the kind of people who could be counted on to be courageous when courage is called for.

It is notable, too, that people who are addicted to this kind of risky behavior generally deny being reckless and instead emphasize all the safety precautions they take. But they should also acknowledge that every single time they engage in their activity, they increase the odds that at some time, they will be injured or killed by it. Instead, they act as if they believe that every time they engage in it without being harmed, it becomes less likely that they ever will be. "I had performed that trick a thousand times, but for some reason that day I miscalculated."

Now I think we can see at least a partial explanation why there is a widespread difference between attitudes towards risky drug taking and attitudes towards other kinds of risky behavior, such as participating in extreme sports. It is because we associate the risks voluntarily taken by mountain-climbers, off-roaders, sky-divers, etc. with the risks voluntarily taken by soldiers, firefighters, and police in situations that require courage. It is hard to think of a situation in which someone needs to take a drug to save someone else's life or other valued property, but not so hard to think of a case where someone needs to climb a mountain, drive into the wilderness, or jump out of a plane with a parachute to do so. The habitual drunkard or heroin addict has made himself or herself unfit for such action, but the extreme sports enthusiast is the fittest of all – as long as he or she lasts.

These considerations might help explain why, for example, it is illegal to take heroin but legal to do an acrobatic loop after riding a motorcycle off the end of a ramp, but they don't justify this different treatment. For that, we would need a convincing argument that would show a) that outlawing the production, sale, and use of heroin is the best method of protecting people from the harm that it is likely to cause them, and b) that any such paternalistic protection of non-drug daredevils, through legal prohibition of their equipment and activities, would be wrong.

But there are other virtues besides courage, and the value of courage depends on other values. What is worth defending? Life and the beauty in which we swim. We can be grateful for the courage of the man or woman of action and also be grateful for another kind of courage, the courage of contemplative people. The risks they face are not so much physical as social, psycho-logical, spiritual. They risk the dangers of social isolation, of falling into fanaticism or other types of mental illness, of becoming lost. But the rewards they seek and sometimes achieve – intellectual honesty, spiritual integrity, loving kindness – are the ones that ground the value of every kind of courage.

I don't think even the very dangerous drug heroin should be illegal, because I think that only makes it more dangerous. Despite the fact that some excellent artists and musicians have been heroin addicts, I haven't seen any evidence that the heroin experience is productive of any insights or breakthroughs that would justify the risks involved. The temporary obliteration of all pain, which is what I understand heroin to produce (I have never tried it and have no desire to do so.) may well be desirable in a medical emergency, but I don't see how the habitual repetition of it could ever lead to a happy outcome. Instead, it is universally acknowledged that it leads to addiction such that it becomes required just for life to be tolerable.

I've been discussing heroin as the exemplar of an illegal non-psychedelic drug. The same things I've said about it could be said about other drugs of the same type, that is, central nervous system depressants. Another type, stimulants, such as cocaine and methamphetamine, are equally addictive, less dangerous in terms of death from an accidental overdose, but more dangerous in terms of health consequences other than that. The important point, though, is that, as with heroin, there seems to be little evidence that these super-stimulants (in comparison to caffeine, a mild stimulant) help people achieve artistic, intellectual, or spiritual insights.

With psychedelics, it's a different story. In direct contrast with heroin, there is a very large margin of safety between effective dose and potentially lethal dose. In this respect, LSD and marijuana are the safest psychedelics (counting marijuana as a mild psychedelic). In respect of the possibility of death from accidental overdose, they are roughly 100 times safer than alcohol, while heroin is twice as dangerous as alcohol. They are also much safer in this respect than many common, over-the-counter medications, such as acetaminophen and aspirin. As for addiction, these types of drugs do not cause the classic addiction where withdrawal of the drug causes physical illness. If by "addiction" we just mean "habitual use," as with moderate drinkers who might, say, have a glass of wine with dinner each day, then the milder of them, particularly marijuana, may be addictive in this sense. However, LSD is, if anything, anti-addictive. That is, frequency of usage tends to taper off over time, naturally and without any struggle, to the point that it is rarely or never used again.

The dangers of a psychedelic such as LSD are not physical, but psychological. LSD can cause confusion, anxiety, panic reactions. An LSD trip can be an intensely unpleasant experience, and in some cases can cause people to hurt themselves in the false belief that it has given them god-like control over everything. Nothing is swept under the rug. A person on an LSD trip will live through the consequences of his or her philosophical and religious beliefs. Any irrational compromise designed to avoid thinking about things one is afraid or ashamed of gets turned into a morality play in which one finds oneself acting. Every false belief is contradicted by intense experience that cannot be ignored.

On the other hand, most people aren't such terrible philosophers that they will be guaranteed to have nothing but bad trips. Every bit of honesty, every positive emotion, every whiff of greatness is equally intensely and intricately lived through. That is why many people, I among them, say that taking LSD was one of the most important things they have ever done, and that an LSD trip can be a religious experience in the truest sense of the words.

"Yes, but it isn't real" is a standard objection, to which I reply with a question, "Why are you willing to accept the reality of the occasional bad consequences of taking LSD – the people who are frightened out of their wits, or who descend into psychoses – but unwilling to accept the reality of the good consequences – the people who say that is has changed their lives for the better? If they are both unreal, the bad consequences along with the good, then there is no reason for LSD to be illegal, since it can't cause any bad consequences that are real. If they are both real, then we need to think about ways to reduce the likelihood of the bad consequences while allowing the good ones.

It is encouraging that more and more people are coming to

see that legally punishing drug use – even clearly harmful drug use – generally causes more harm than it prevents. It is also important for people to know that LSD and LSD-like drugs (e.g., mescaline, psilocybin, DMT), when used with due caution, can cause healing, religious experiences. I know of no evidence that any other illegal drugs do so, with the possible exception of marijuana, which in any case clearly does have medicinal properties. It is unhelpful to the cause of human happiness and spiritual progress that legislators, on one side, and rock stars and other celebrities, on the other, are ignorant of the stark differences between psychedelics and drugs like heroin, cocaine, methamphetamine, PCP, etc., thereby setting a horrible example for other uneducated people. People need to know that super stimulants, like cocaine and methamphetamine, and super sedatives, like heroin and barbiturates, should be used only under competent medical supervision. Otherwise, they are not good for you. The same goes for muscle relaxants and anti-depressants that can be legally prescribed. The widely socially acceptable and legal drugs, caffeine (stimulant) and alcohol (sedative), should be used with due caution and mindfulness, keeping in mind that alcohol especially is for some people as addictive and harmful as any illegal drug, as is the increasingly legally restricted new social pariah, tobacco (combination stimulant and sedative). But alcohol in moderation has some health benefits, while tobacco, even in moderation, is unhealthy.

I hope it is clear, then, that the "Psychedelic" half of the label "Psychedelic Christian" that I attach to the world view I'm recommending is not intended in any way to glamorize libertinism about drugs. Neither do I want to endorse a punitive attitude towards users of drugs of which I personally disapprove. Here I just want to acknowledge the fact that psychedelic drugs have caused profound, healing, life-changing experiences for many people, including me.

I have heard people argue that taking a drug cannot cause a

genuine religious experience, because if an experience is caused by a drug, then we know it is not caused by God or a Higher Power or Transcendent Being. However, I haven't heard a clear explanation of how we know that. It sounds to me suspiciously like the "knowledge" that nothing good comes out of Galilee.

Along these lines, too, I recall reading an anti-psychedelic argument that remarked on the necessity of a long period of devotional practices to achieve a genuine religious experience. The writer compared the non-drug-induced experience to reaching the summit of a mountain through a difficult climb, while he compared a drug-induced mystical experience to being dropped off on the summit by a helicopter. The view from the top might be the same, but the sense of achievement would be missing. To this I would reply that the critic should apply the empiricist principle: try it and see for yourself. Yes, the fact that one can decide to take a pill and have an LSD trip is the thing that is new compared to the era before Hoffman discovered LSD, but anyone who has done so knows that in the experience that follows the faster the ride to the top, the greater the demands on all of one's psychological and spiritual resources. It's like an eternity of devotional practice. That is why it gets harder and harder to decide to do it, as one realizes, as one did not at first, what one is committing oneself to. I seem to remember that it can be easy, too. "My yoke is easy. My burden is light." Nevertheless, it has been decades now since my last trip and maybe I will never take another one.

One of the things I learned the hard way was that doing it because someone else wants you to, for whatever reason, is the royal road to a bad trip.

There are experiences of great value that you can't get any other way, but since that value lasts a lifetime, there is no need to repeat it. That isn't to say that it is necessarily wrong to repeat it if you want to. But I do also frankly confess that I am afraid of it too. "Fear of the Lord is the beginning of wisdom." There is something about the responsibility that you incur by deliberately deciding to take a trip that makes it daunting.

Like all scientific discoveries, the discovery of LSD and other psychedelics gives us more predictive power and control than we had before. One can simply swallow a dose and be sure to have an extraordinary experience. Now we know how to produce an extraordinary experience of a particular kind, whereas we didn't know before. Even more importantly, given the right set and setting, one can pretty much guarantee a religious experience. However, as I argued in *God is a Symbol of Something True,* religion has to do with facing the fact that there are important things that are outside one's control, and this is no less true of psychedelic religion than of any other kind. Transcending the fear of loss of control by realizing the extent to which one never has been in control is one way of describing what is religious about a psychedelic trip. But there is no guarantee that that process will be pleasant. All that is guaranteed is that it will be overwhelming, but not whether one will experience being overwhelmed as a liberating delight accompanied by angels singing, "Glory, glory, glory!" or as an anxiety ridden struggle with the Devil, filled with dark suspicions and a constant mocking sarcastic undertone. It is also possible for a single trip to contain both ways of experiencing the confrontation with the way things are in all their richness. Either way, the gradual lessening of the effects of the drug comes as a beneficial resolution. Either way, one has gained by the experience, and these gains are never really lost, which is why the question of how often and how many times to repeat the experience takes care of itself.

In the old days I was annoyed by Alan Watts's saying, "When you get the message, hang up the phone." I thought, "I got the message, but I like to be reminded." If you can remember what it is of which you want to be reminded, you don't need to be reminded. Nevertheless, you may still want to be reminded. And there is the distinction between remembering what something was like and actually experiencing it again.

I was also unpersuaded by those who argued that because they had tried both psychedelics and _____ (Fill in the blank with: following a Hindu guru, or following Jesus, or Zen meditation, or Sufi mysticism, or...) and preferred _____, this showed that _____ really was better. I'm not trying to persuade anyone to take a psychedelic trip or not to take a psychedelic trip. I'm trying only to remind those who have forgotten (if that is possible), and inform those who don't know, of the religious nature of psychedelic trips. Even if you never take another psychedelic trip, and, even if you never have and never will, it is important to know this. Of course, I don't think you can fully appreciate it if you never have the experience for yourself. I have nothing against those who don't do it because they're afraid to do it or because they simply have no desire to do it, for whatever reason. After all, I presently belong to one or the other of those two classes. I waver as to which one. But I do take issue with anyone who mocks and sneers at the claim that psychedelic drugs cause religious experiences.

How is all this supposed to win over a Christian who is made nervous by talk of the religious nature of psychedelic experience? I hope such a person will understand, from the inside, the desire to act consistently with a religious conviction, and will thus consider that maybe there is something to this after all. How is it supposed to win over someone who has heretofore rejected both Christianity and psychedelic enthusiasm? It is just an appeal from one open mind to another.

Christianity

It is now time to address those, whether psychedelic veterans or not, who don't believe in Christianity. My guess is that most of you are unconvinced of any form of theism, although there may be some of you who have flown to the moon on gossamer wings and yet remain committed Jews or Muslims. I don't have a quarrel with any of you. Until quite recently, I counted myself among those who believe that psychedelic experience is religious or, if you prefer, spiritual, but that it is more compatible with non-theistic Asian religious views, such as Advaita (non-dualistic) Vedanta, Taoism, or Zen Buddhism, than it is with any variety of theism.

By a few years ago, when I wrote *God is a Symbol of Something True*, I had moved in the direction of theism, and I used the common sense distinction between symbolism and literalism to try to make it clear that I was arguing for a symbolic theism that is not a scientific hypothesis about the origin of the universe. I declined to identify as a Christian, while expressing the hope that the view for which I argued was consistent with true Christianity. Since then, I have joined the First Congregational Church of Los Angeles, so now I do identify myself as a Christian, a psychedelic, Taoistic Christian.

When I was addressing those of you who may or may not be Christians and who don't believe in psychedelics, I challenged you with the empiricist principle, "Try it and see for yourself," implying that I have tried it and seen for myself, and that you can, too. Now that I'm addressing those of you who may or may not believe in psychedelics but who in any case don't believe in theism, I'm saying again, "Try it and see for yourself," only this time I am still in the process of trying to see for myself if I have a clear enough understanding of what the basic theistic propositions mean, in the experiential sense. By "the basic theistic propo-

94

sitions," I mean the propositions that there is a God who creates the universe and that he loves each and every one of us.

It's interesting to contrast the strikingly different ways in which following that advice seems hard or easy in the two cases. In one way, it's as easy as pie to swallow a pill. This has often been used as a criticism of psychedelic drug use by those who are psychedelically naïve and who think that a psychedelic trip is a sort of souped up joy ride of empty thrills. "Don't take the easy way out. Don't try to escape reality by taking psychedelic drugs," these unsophisticated critics have said. Those who are experienced, however, know that if they are contemplating another psychedelic trip, they had better be prepared to face heaven or hell in their immediate future; that it doesn't get any realer than this, and that deciding to go to church on Sunday morning instead would be a light burden indeed by comparison.

On the other hand, it is easier at least to know just what you are supposed to do to try and see for yourself whether psychedelics cause religious experiences than it is in the case of trying and seeing for yourself whether the theistic propositions are true. You just educate yourself as well as you can about what to expect, set up a situation that is as little likely as possible to cause you discomfort or anxiety, and take the pill. When it comes to theism, however, it isn't so clear what you are supposed to do to try it and see for yourself whether it is true. How can you just decide to believe something you don't believe in order to see if you should believe it?

There is a God who creates the universe and he loves each and every one of us. Do I believe this or not? I said "creates" rather than "created," because I think of the universe as everything that has been, is, or will be going on all at once everywhere, rather than as in the more static formulation, "everything that exists." I've never been terribly interested in the question, how did the universe come into existence, as if we are assuming there was a time in the past when nothing existed, and then we have to explain how out of that situation it came about that something did exist after all. I've never found persuasive those who argue that there must be a God in order to explain how everything came into existence. I think the answer to the fundamental metaphysical question, why is there something rather than nothing, is that there is no possible world in which anyone has the true thought that nothing exists, because, of course, both the person entertaining the proposition "Nothing exists" and the proposition itself would exist and so the proposition would be false. Even if there were no thinkers, there must exist in every world at least one thing in order for that world to be a world at all; that is, in all possible worlds, at least one thing exists; that is, it is necessarily true that there is something and not nothing.

Now someone might reply that the answer that says that God created the universe out of nothing isn't based on the assumption that there was once a time when nothing at all existed. Someone who argues that there must be a God to explain why the universe exists is assuming that God always existed. So, we are in agreement that there has always been something, or, in this case, Someone. This in turn invites the response that it would be simpler just to assume that the universe has always existed. That way we can try to understand the universe scientifically in a clearer way than we can if we treat the hypothesis that God created the universe as a kind of quasi-scientific hypothesis. The problem is that if God did it, we have to admit that we don't understand how he did it, so it isn't clear what our hypothesis is.

In the past I have tried to explain this in terms of a distinction between a literal and a symbolic interpretation of the claim that God created (past tense) the universe. The literal interpretation would be one in which this claim is treated as the best explanation of the origin of the universe, beating out alternatives such as the Big Bang theory (unless the Big Bang is thought of as God's method) or a theory in terms of multiple universes. The symbolic interpretation would be that the story of Genesis symbolizes the primacy of intelligence and love in creating value in the universe by representing these personal qualities as actually existing prior to the universe itself. But this would be only a symbol of the literal truth that the universe has always existed in some form or other, whether as an infinitely dense singularity or as an ever increasingly rapidly expanding system of spacetime destined for heat death, and that love and intelligence are always there potentially but are actualized only at those spacetime moments when/where intelligent beings exist and love each other. It's like saying that those are the moments that count and all the others are there so that they may be there.

The distinction between symbolism and literalism is clearest in regard to the parables. A literal interpretation of the parable of the prodigal son, for example, would insist that one must accept literally, historically, that there was a young man who went away, wasted his fortune, came back repentant, and was welcomed by his father, to the consternation of his jealous brother who had stayed at home and been obedient. A symbolic interpretation would be that it doesn't matter whether there really was a particular young man who did those things. What matters is what the story tells us about how God loves us. But that distinction is not so clear in regard to the main propositions of theism, that there is a God who creates the world and that he loves each and every one of us. What would be the literal interpretation that could be peeled away from the symbolic one? Or what would be the symbolic interpretation that could be separated from the literal one? Martin Luther said something like this, "All around God it rains and snows miracles." It seems the wrong question to ask if he meant that literally or symbolically.

Nevertheless, that literal vs. symbolic contrast, with a preference for the symbolic interpretation, is the best I've been able to do when considering the theistic proposition about creation in the past tense: God created the universe. Now suppose we change it as I've suggested, to the present tense: God creates the universe, and he does it at every moment. This isn't a quasi-scientific hypothesis to compete with scientific cosmogonical theories like the Big Bang. It is more like the explanation for the existence of a work of art. An experiential appreciation for a great work of art is categorically different from any kind of scientific account, whether one of the physical basis of the artist and the work, or a sociological or psychological theory about how the work came about. This doesn't imply that an aesthetic appreciation of a work of art or of the world is in any way inconsistent with a true scientific account. The chemical composition of the paint an artist uses, for example, isn't magically transformed because of the way the painter has applied it to the canvas. The magical transformation is in the appreciative viewer's ability to see the world in a new way.

There was a time when there was no Fifth Symphony by Beethoven. That musical genius thought it up. Or, consider the case of William Blake composing the poems, "The Lamb" and "The Tyger." How do we understand artistic inspiration? I suppose certain mental images came before Blake's mind. It was maybe as if he heard a voice in his mind saying certain words. He played around with them, tried out variations, worked at it, and eventually hit on the beauty and perfection of those poems. I have some idea of how great artists create their works, although if I really understood it, I'd do it myself. Perhaps this is the way to understand, in some dim way, the theistic proposition that God creates the universe, creates it anew every moment. He can't contain himself. He thinks it up. He is inspired. It is oozing, flowing, welling up, on the surface and underneath. It is falling from the sky, squeezing through every crack, booming and buzzing, and as gentle as a breeze. I know I'm not in control of all those, and neither is this the collective work of a committee of human beings. God is the Great Artist or Magician. He conjures every moment into existence.

A scientific explanation is in terms of how each moment is caused by the conditions that existed during the moment just before, which in turn is caused by the moment just before that one, which in turn... leading back to the Big Bang or, conceivably (but not in an empirically testable way) to whatever caused the Big Bang. But as Hume so convincingly argued, there is no logical necessity to any of those causal connections: at every moment, it is perfectly conceivable that the expected outcome will not occur and that something else will happen instead. Notice that I didn't say it was perfectly reasonable but just that it is conceivable. It is unreasonable to expect a well-established pattern to change for no apparent reason. But it is also unreasonable to think that it just can't happen. And I suspect that it happens much more often than we are aware of, our lack of awareness of it being due to the inattention and forgetfulness that gives us a false sense of security laid over a dread of catastrophe. We can give up that false security and see our dread of catastrophe as a manifestation of a fear of miracles. Where Hume went wrong, as the British philosopher H. H. Price has pointed out, was in persuading himself and others into thinking "that the word 'miracle' just means 'an event which is inconsistent with causal laws'. But all it meant originally," Price has objected, "was 'a wonder', a surprising or extraordinary event."[10] The fact that an event is surprising or extraordinary is perfectly consistent with its having a causal explanation. What matters, from a religious point of view, is the surprise and wonder.

The same faulty conception that Hume articulated may be behind the confusion exhibited by some people on acid who have hurt and in some cases killed themselves by jumping out of trees or buildings:

1   A miracle just happened.
2   A miracle is an event which is inconsistent with the laws of

nature. Therefore,

3 The laws of nature have been suspended. Therefore,

4 It is just as likely that I can flap my arms and fly as it is that I will fall.

This is a deductively valid but unsound logical argument, unsound because premise (2) is false. In the future, please don't ignore what I just said. IT IS IMPORTANT!

Some of the visionary experiences I've had on psychedelic trips have been more beautiful, complex, surprising, and deeply moving and personal than even the greatest works of art I've ever experienced. But who is the artist? All I know is that it is not my conscious self. It might make sense in a way to say that I'm doing it, but not in the sense that I am doing it and you aren't. We are all doing and being done, and God, I suppose, is the doing that gets us done. Why is that not nature? Because nature is the way things are, and I'm thinking about what seems to be a conscious, supremely artistic activity that results in things being the way they are. When you really "get" a work of art, you understand it as something being communicated to you by another mind.

Then why the "seems to be"? Are you willing or are you not to affirm that the universe, reality, nature, the whole world, including you and me, brothers and sisters, is the artistic creation of the mind of God? Well, yes I am, if you will allow me to insist that it is a metaphor for something that I can completely feel but cannot completely understand. I remember one day at the Huntington, while viewing an exhibition of drawings by artists associated with the Pre-Raphaelite movement, I was gazing at a particular drawing, of a mill on a stream or a bridge – I have only a vague memory of the image now. What I do recall vividly was the feeling that came like a flash of insight, of being in direct contact with the mind of that artist, who died before I was born and about whom I knew very little. In front of my eyes at that moment was a piece of thick paper on which he had drawn lines that pictured a pleasing scene that he had gazed upon on a day many years ago. Now when I say that the scene itself that he gazed upon, along with all the scenes that any of us ever gaze upon, are the artistic creation of the mind of God, I'm just saying that it's something like the creation of that drawing by that artist. I'm not claiming to have anywhere near as clear an understanding as I do of how another human being can see things in a way very similar to the way I see things, although he or she may see things I haven't seen and may help me to notice things I otherwise wouldn't have noticed, and can make marks on paper and thereby convey that to me. For one thing, I'm not clear as to whether God's art is representational of a reality that transcends the universe itself, as the drawing represents a scene that is not itself a drawing, or whether instead God's art, i.e., the world, is non-representational like the absolute music of a great composer, so that the world just tells us great things about what it is to be divine the way a great piece of music tells us great things about what it is to be human. By the way, since being human is part of the world – and the most important part to us – being human also tells us something about being divine. But it isn't just being human in a general sense; it is living one's own individual life, which is an art that each one of us can practice.

* * *

Living one's life isn't something that can be achieved once and for all, as any other work of art can be. It is a lifelong project. I hope that this book plays some small role in that process for you, as it does for me.

At the moment I want to say more about why I now believe I am a Christian, whereas for many years up until just a few years ago, I didn't. First of all, I've been persuaded by what I've read and thought about the subject – for example, the writings of Albert Schweitzer, Alfred North Whitehead, and Charles

Hartshorne – that Christianity itself is an ongoing process rather than a set of supposedly final answers to be either accepted or rejected. Secondly, I've found through experience that Christian worship and fellowship is deeply appealing to me. This is my answer to the "sins of Christianity" objection, which I think is what inspires those who want to make a distinction between being religious and being spiritual and to reserve their commitments to the latter. I agree that people have done horrible things to other people in the name of Christianity, especially in the periods when there has been a blurry distinction or none at all between church and state. I agree that Christians have gone wrong in conceiving of God in the image of a powerful dictator. I agree that Christians should atone for centuries of making enemies of Jews. But so do more and more Christians. I like church. It has beautiful art, music, architecture, rituals that remind us of the beauty of life, and people who are trying to understand and practice what life is all about in the deepest sense. Of course, some churches do a better job of this than others.

Whitehead especially has helped me conceive of worship in a way that is attractive rather than repellent as it used to be to me. The repellent version is a kind of showy self-abnegation grudgingly disguising a conceited despisal and jealously of non-believers, before a God who demands it as a tyrant demands obedience and tribute. The following passage from *Process and Reality* expresses the contrast between "worship" in this sense and the genuine article:

> Such order as we find in nature is never force – it presents itself as the one harmonious adjustment of complex detail. Evil is the brute motive force of fragmentary purpose, disregarding the eternal vision. Evil is overruling, retarding, hurting. The power of God is the worship that He inspires. (p. 192)

But, you say, the historical Christian creeds, such as the Apostle's Creed, the Nicene Creed, the Athanasian Creed, certainly sound like a set of final answers either to be accepted or rejected. And so do some of the sayings of Jesus, especially in the Gospel of John, and some of the writings of St. Paul.

My reply is that Jesus' message was one of reinterpretation and revitalization of tradition. It seemed like a rejection of that tradition to the scribes and Pharisees, but Jesus clearly stated that it wasn't. Christianity is all about birth, the coming of the kingdom of heaven, and life, life, everlasting life. God is a living god. Only dead things can be pinned down.

But reinterpretation and revitalization of tradition is not rejection of tradition. If we invented a whole new language, for a long time we would need to translate it into the old one in order to understand it. Tradition and ritual is a kind of beauty that can only come into being over centuries. Gothic architecture, stained glass windows, organ and choral music, ritual processions and recessions, candles and incense are ways that humans have discovered to evoke the sacred, and it would be foolish to reject them on the grounds that they are old, but Christianity is a living religion, and life is ever new. Of course, it would not be foolish to replace such elements with something better or equally good. I was surprised to discover, for example, while living for a few months in London teaching in a study abroad program, that I felt even more inspired and spiritually at home while taking communion at St. Paul's, with its relatively more modern, open and light-filled English Baroque architecture, than I did attending evensong surrounded by the ancient Gothic majesty of the interior of Westminster Abbey.

It is a truism that a church is not a building, but that doesn't take away from the importance of a sacred place, and it is undeniable that great architecture has been and continues to be dedicated to the service of Christian worship, as is also true of the work of gifted craftsmen, painters, composers and musicians, and writers.

That isn't to say that art needs to be expressly dedicated to Christian worship or to any kind of worship in order to do the sacred job of extending and intensifying the experience of Beauty. Whether the artist is a Christian, an atheist, a Hindu, a Jew, a secular humanist, or whatever, doesn't matter. All that matters is whether the artist has succeeded in reminding us yet again of the deep beauty that is always there.

Even considered purely as art, the Gospels achieve a perfection that hasn't been surpassed.

* * *

One night, a few days after writing that next-to-last paragraph about the beauty that is always there, I dreamed I was in the presence of an amazingly beautiful, intelligent, graceful woman, and that I was becoming aware that she deeply and tenderly loved me in a way that she loved no one else. And I loved her and was so grateful for her love. She was gentle, good, and wise, and ravishingly beautiful, like a fairy tale princess or queen, and it was hard for me to believe at first that she had chosen me, although she also made it unmistakably clear that she did. There were also some other women present part of the time who were her friends and confidantes, and who reassured me that it was so. What followed very shortly, so quickly that it was almost simultaneous, was that I also knew that she was dying, and then, very soon, that she had in fact died. This all seemed as real to me as what I am experiencing right now.

An indefinite amount of time passed before I woke up and realized that it was a dream. As I lay there awake, barely emerged from the dream, I was thinking how the woman could be Jesus, or the Holy Spirit, or God, and, at the same time, my wife. In the dream, I was amazed that out of all the people she could have chosen, she chose me. She adored me every bit as much as I adored her, and in being loved by her, I had everything I could ever possibly want. In the dream she died, as Jesus died, and it was as inescapable as every death, and I was so sad, and I was thinking, as I was waking up, that the love of the woman in the dream is also my wife's love for me, and my love and happiness in the dream is my love for my wife and the way she makes me happy. That the woman in the dream died reminds me what a heavy loss it will be if my wife dies before me. We are each fully mortal as well as fully immortal. Grief over loss is just as authentic and true to life as is the joy of falling in love. The true joy of being alive and in love contains the true sorrow over death, and vice-versa. Jesus died a real death, but he was resurrected, and his love for each of us is not abstract or vague love for humanity or all living creatures in general. He is the shepherd who has lost one sheep out of a hundred and who drops everything, risking losing some more of the ninety-nine safe sheep, in order to find that one. He is the woman in my dream, who loved me in particular. He is present in the way my wife loves me and in the way I love her. No one can ever replace her.

In order for Christianity to work for me, I find I must think of God's love for each and every one of us as not only parental love, to which we respond with filial love, not only love of friend for friend, but also romantic and erotic love, the love of two people intoxicated with the living presence of each other. God's love is not a separate thing in addition to, or somehow greater than, our love for each other. It is our love for each other, and it is thereby as transcendent as you please, for that is exactly how we transcend ourselves at the same moment that we are most authentically ourselves. We often fall short of or betray that ideal, but we forever renew our quest for it.

The reality of selves

No one can ever replace her. Here is a clear case where we see that you can't separate the most emotional, personal side of religion from the kinds of perplexing questions philosophers concern themselves with. As I have mentioned, reading works by Whitehead and by Hartshorne has enriched my view of Christianity as a living religion that can be thoroughly consistent with the findings of science and just as open-ended and accepting of novelty. This is one reason I'm not overly worried that maybe I shouldn't call myself a Christian even if someone who regards himself or herself as a defender of the orthodox Christian view would want to find something wrong with my reasoning concerning what an afterlife might be like and the probability that there is also a pre-life. I find persuasive Whitehead's comparison of Buddhism and Christianity:

Buddhism is the most colossal example in history of applied metaphysics.

Christianity took the opposite road. It has always been a religion seeking a metaphysic, in contrast to Buddhism which is a metaphysic generating a religion. The defect of a metaphysical system is the very fact that it is a neat little system of thought, which thereby oversimplifies its expression of the world. Christianity has, in its historical development, struggled with another difficulty, namely, the fact that it has no clear-cut separation from the crude fancies of the older tribal religions.[11]

In the development of his own metaphysical system, Whitehead certainly strove to avoid oversimplification. He got so many important things right that I would like to believe he got everything right; and the difficulty of always understanding exactly what he means, especially in the large portions of his works that are highly abstract and terminologically inventive, makes me shy to say that he didn't. Nevertheless, I can only make progress by trying to make clear what I now think, and I think I see a problem with his analysis of reality as constituted by actual occasions of perceptivity so that a person is a society of such occasions, with no absolute self-identity through time.

In *Process and Reality* Whitehead wrote:

> The subjectivist principle is that the whole universe consists of elements disclosed in the analysis of subjects. Process is the becoming of experience. It follows that the philosophy of organism entirely accepts the subjectivist bias of modern philosophy. It also accepts Hume's doctrine that nothing is to be received into the philosophical scheme which is not discoverable as an element in subjective experience. This is the ontological principle.

I have two comments. One is that I would say that, since Whitehead wrote this, there has been a change in the bias among philosophers. At least in Anglo-American philosophy there is, if anything, an objectivist bias. The second is that the problem is that Hume did not think the subject is given in subjective experience. I think he was wrong about that, and I am not sure that Whitehead would agree with me. Experience is given as a series of discrete passing moments or events or, in Whitehead's terminology, "actual occasions," each of which becomes the history of its successor. But did Whitehead also believe, as I do, that it is also given from a first-person perspective that is one among many and that is always this one and never any of the others? Whether he did or not, this is the view that I want to defend.

When we think about objects of experience, language implies

that there is a substance that has properties. The ball is red, is roughly spherical, is rubbery, is soft. But this metaphysics that language implies, of a substratum underlying its properties, turns the substratum itself into something that is not experienced. We only experience the properties. Experience is always of a process, not of an unchanging substance underlying the observed changes. In this case, then, language is misleading if we use it to support a metaphysical view that is not based on experience.

Experience tells us that the things that are always the same are not things like the ball itself, which is supposed to be something that is never itself experienced and that underlies and is separate from its redness, its roughly spherical shape, etc., and which is supposed to stay the same even if these properties change (if it is painted white, for example). The kinds of things that are always the same are things like a particular shade of red, which may recur in many different experiences, but itself is always the same and is actually experienced every time it enters into an actual occasion. Whitehead calls these "eternal objects."

The term "first-person perspective" is based on the grammatical distinction between first-person (I, me, my, mine, we, us, our, ours), second-person (you, your, yours), and third-person (he, him, his, she, her, hers, it, its, they, them, their, theirs) ways of referring to people, animals, and things. Here again, language implies that there is something – call it the subject of experiences – that is separate from what is observed in experience. I see the ball, and I am not the ball, and I am not my act of seeing the ball. I am the one who is doing the seeing. If someone else also sees the ball, I am not the one doing that seeing. I am the subject of my act of seeing, and you are the subject of your act of seeing, and he is the subject of his act of seeing, etc. Hume and his followers think that, in this case also, what language implies will give us a false metaphysical view that is not supported by experience. Hume famously wrote:

There are some philosophers who imagine we are every moment intimately conscious of what we call our Self; that we feel its existence; and are certain, beyond the evidence of a demonstration, both of its perfect identity and simplicity...

For my part, when I enter most intimately into what I call *myself*, I always stumble on some particular perception or other, of heat or cold, light or shade, love or hatred, pain or pleasure. I never can catch *myself* at any time without a perception, and never can observe anything but the perception.[12]

Hume goes on to explain the concept of personal identity as confusion between identity and a succession of closely related objects, and draws the conclusion that a person is "a bundle or collection of different perceptions." Interestingly, in the Appendix to the Treatise, he expresses his dissatisfaction with his explanation:

In short there are two principles, which I cannot render consistent; nor is it in my power to renounce either one of them, viz. *that all our distinct perceptions are distinct existences,* and *that the mind never perceives any real connection among distinct existences.*[13]

Why are these two principles inconsistent? That is not obvious to me. However, I think what Hume is getting at is that if both principles are true, the second one is only trivially true. On Hume's view the mind itself is just a succession of distinct existences, and if it never perceives any real connection among distinct existences, then there is no way to account for the connections among perceptions that make them a bundle, i.e., a mind. Then the mind never perceives any real connections among distinct existences, all right, because the mind never perceives anything, because there is no such thing as a mind in the first place. At this point Hume simply says, "For my part, I must plead the privilege of a sceptic, and confess, that this difficulty is too hard for my understanding."

I think Whitehead may be among those philosophers who follow Hume's explanation of personal identity as consisting of a succession of distinct perceptions without realizing, as Hume himself did, that it is not satisfactory. At least he is if one of his interpreters, John B Cobb, Jr. has interpreted him correctly.[14]

But is it true that the self, or what I've been calling "the first-person perspective," is not given in experience? I claim that it is not true. Unlike the case in which the convenient shorthand of language may mislead us into positing an unchanging substratum that underlies changing properties but that itself cannot be experienced, the first-person perspective that is expressed in language corresponds to something that is given in experience. If it weren't, we would have to say that the true metaphysical view is that there is simply no way for anyone to know which subject of experiences, out of all the subjects there are, he or she is. But clearly we do know it. Experience shows that although we can both see the same sunset, my seeing it and your seeing it are two different events, for I can close my eyes while yours are still open, and then my seeing it stops while yours goes on.

I learn from experience over time that other people don't always have the same sensations that I do. I don't in the same way learn from experience over time which sensations I am feeling. That is something that is just given immediately in any one experience at a time. Hume seems to think that the only thing given immediately in experience is a bare perception not yet attributable to any particular point of view, so that it could just as well be something experienced only by you as something experienced only by me or by someone else. And then he thinks it is his job to produce a theory that will explain what counts as a bundle that constitutes a mind. And even if he could explain that, he would still be left with the question of how any bundle identifies itself among all the possible bundles. But no perception ever occurs as if from no point of view. The point of view is just as immediately given as the perception considered as an object. If you object that the concept of a point of view is not immediately given, I would agree but point out that neither is the concept of a perception. What is immediately given is not the concept but the instantiation of the concept.

There can be problems about whether or not a particular description applies to me. For example, a friend might show me a photograph and tell me that I am the third person from the left. But I don't remember the occasion and don't recognize any of the other people, and am not sure that the person who is supposed to be me really looks like I looked. In contrast, there is never any problem about whether or not I am presently having this particular experience, even though if I try to describe it so as to do justice to it, I inevitably find myself distracted by some new experience, which is also immediately given as from my point of view.

I was led into this discussion by consideration of the statement, "No one can replace her." What is it about her that cannot be replaced? What is it about any of us that cannot be replaced? What do we lose when someone we love dies? Part of the answer would be the role that he or she played in our lives, but that is something that could potentially be replaced. If a beloved pet dies, the master could get a new pet which in many ways could be just as good or better. A widow or widower could remarry. Parents who have lost a child can in some cases have another child. But we realize that it is no bad reflection on such replacements to believe also that there is something that they can never replace. What is it? What is it about you that makes you you? I think it is your first-person perspective on the world. If you have died, you no longer have a first-person perspective in this world, so that is what is going to be missing, no matter how excellently someone else might take your place in this world. When we love someone, there are many things about him or her that at least conceivably, in principle, could be duplicated. The fact that the spouse of an identical twin does not in the same way love the twin sister or brother, shows that there is something else that can't be duplicated that is loved. I propose that it is the first-person perspective of the person who is loved, which just comes to saying that it is the person himself or herself.

There are quite a few philosophers since Hume who dispute this. They continue to think that it is just as mistaken to believe in an enduring subject of experiences as it to believe in an unobservable substance that underlies all its observable properties. One of them, Derek Parfit, is an excellent writer who uses ingenious science-fiction-style examples to support what he calls a Reductionist View of personal identity. In this final section, I shall contrast my view with Parfit's and leave it for you to judge.

I have made some statements that imply I am a non-reductionist about personal identity, for example, that you are always absolutely you, and that no one can replace my wife. If reductionists about personal identity are correct, it isn't true that no one can replace her. On any reductionist account of personal identity, what I am, what you are, what she is, in each case is just a series of replacements, and so there is no reason why one series itself could not be replaced by another, as long as there are enough intermediate steps so that this becomes just another, longer series of replacements.

To see why a philosopher might be moved to entertain the proposition that a person is a series of events, we can begin with the hypothesis that a person's identity over a period of time consists in the continued existence of the same body over that same period of time. We understand right away that this cannot mean simply the continued existence of one and the same physical object, unmoved and unchanged over time. A living human body is an organism that is continually incorporating various solids, liquids, and gases and excreting others, growing new cells and sloughing off old ones, with all the parts associated together so as to maintain that life until such time as injury, disease, or gradual decay leads to a loss of the right kind of organization to sustain life. Thus a person's existence over a lifetime would consist of a series of groups of physical events associated in such a way as to preserve, from moment to moment in the series, vital biological functions. From moment to moment, one such set of associated events would be replaced by another.

But a purely physical/biological account like that would make the doctrine of reincarnation or transmigration not only false but inconceivable, since reincarnation, by hypothesis, would be the beginning of a new series of associated physical events discontinuous with the previous series. In other words, it isn't the body that gets reincarnated. This is a problem for the purely physical/biological account because it certainly seems conceivable, for example, that I could wake up one morning and find that I had a different body. A solution would be to propose instead that a person's continued existence consists in a series of mental events where each successor is associated with its predecessor psychologically through memories, the forming and carrying out of intentions, agreement in beliefs and desires, likes and dislikes. Thus, in the case I imagined, of waking up to find I had a different body, I would be one person, who first had one body and then had another, because I would remember having the old body all my life up until that fateful morning; and even though this weird event would upset some of my old beliefs, I would also have beliefs and desires, likes and dislikes, that matched those I had had the day before.

However, since even in that imaginary case, or in a case of transmigration after death, I would still have a body, though a different one, and since in cases of amnesia or dementia, we would need to explain the continued existence of a person in terms of links between physical events rather than psychological ones, we might prefer to combine the two analyses and propose that a person's continued existence consists in a series of physical and/or mental events, associated so as to maintain either biological or psychological continuity, or, most familiarly, both.

Either way, a person would be a series of groups of events being replaced by other groups of events, from one moment to the next. And then it is conceivable that a person could literally be replaced by someone else, in the sense of turning into someone else. This would not be a case of reincarnation, because in reincarnation one and the same person leads many lives. Rather this would be a case of one series of mental and physical events, associated in such a way as to constitute an identifiable person existing over a period of time, being followed in close spatio-temporal proximity by a series of events that no longer constitute the existence of that person, in turn followed by a further series of events that now constitute the existence of a different person.

In *Reasons and Persons* Parfit describes such an imaginary case, not, of course, to show that his Reductionist View implies that this sort of thing is likely to happen, but to argue simply that such a case is conceivable, and the Reductionist View could explain it just as plausibly as it can explain any normal case of the continued existence of a person, while in contrast a defender of a non-reductionist view attempting to explain it would be forced to make some implausible claims.

For the purposes of his argument Parfit asks us to imagine a spectrum of cases in which scientists remove a certain percentage of the cells in his brain and body and replace them with cells that are exact duplicates of cells that were in Greta Garbo's body when she was 30. We are to imagine that the result in each case is a living person, and that exact duplication of a cell, organ, or entire organism results in exact duplication of salient properties of the cell, organ, or entire organism; in other words, that an exact, molecule-by-molecule, cell-by-cell replication of the state of a person's body at a given time will result in a living person who exactly resembles the original person both physically and psychologically.

Parfit makes it clear that he is not claiming this kind of replication is ever likely to happen and admits that is may well be physically impossible. But he defends his use of this kind of science-fiction example as a way of elucidating the implications of our concepts of personal identity, survival, and what matters in survival.

At one end of the spectrum of cases, a team of scientists remove and replace a very small percentage of the total cells in Parfit's body. At the other end, they remove and replace 100% of the cells in his body. Parfit says that it is clear that in the case where the scientists remove and replace just a few cells, the resulting person would be Parfit. He says, too, that in the case where the scientists remove and replace every cell in his body with a cell that is a duplicate of one from Garbo's body, the resulting person would be, not Parfit, but a living replica of Greta Garbo as she was at age 30. But we shouldn't forget the entire spectrum of cases between these two cases at either end. We are to imagine a great number of cases in between, where in each succeeding case, beginning with the initial case of replacing just a few cells, there is each time a just slightly higher percentage of cells removed and replaced, until we reach the case with 100% removal and replacement. Parfit thinks this example of an imaginary spectrum of cases supports his Reductionist View of personal identity, which says that when we have all the facts about the physical and psychological connections between events, there are no more facts to be had about whether a person at one time is identical to a person at another time – so that it is conceivable that there could be a case where there is no deter-minate answer to the question about personal identity, unless we simply arbitrarily stipulate one. His example of the spectrum of cases is designed to imply that conclusion, for he argues that the non-reductionist is committed to saying that even in a case from the middle of this spectrum of cases – where, say, 50% of Parfit's cells are removed and replaced by duplicate Garbo cells – there must be a determinate answer about the identity of the resulting person. This resulting person would be roughly half male and half female. Half of this person's memories and psychological characteristics would resemble Parfit's and the other half Garbo's, and his or her physical appearance would be some kind of half-and-half mixture of resemblance to Parfit and to Garbo. Is this person Parfit, or a duplicate of Garbo, or someone else, neither Parfit nor a replica of Garbo? In this 50/50 case, we would probably be inclined to say that this is neither Parfit nor a duplicate of Garbo, but exactly where in the spectrum of cases would be the last case where the resulting person would be Parfit and the first case where he or she would be neither Parfit nor a duplicate of Garbo? And where would be the last case where he or she would be neither Parfit nor a duplicate of Garbo and the first case where she would be a duplicate of Garbo?

Parfit's argument is that a reductionist about personal identity can shrug off these questions as empty, merely verbal questions. Once we know all the facts about the physical and psychological connections between Parfit and the resulting person and between the latter and Garbo as she was at 30, there is no further fact waiting to be discovered that would enable us to answer this question. In contrast, a non-reductionist, who holds that personal identity is a further fact beyond any analysis in terms of physical and psychological connections between events, will have to explain how any possible answer would differ from merely stipulating a sharp borderline between adjacent cases in the spectrum to give us a determinate answer, in every case, of whether the resulting person is Parfit, neither Parfit nor a duplicate of Garbo, or a duplicate of Garbo. For that matter, the non-reductionist would also be committed to there being a fact about whether a duplicate of Garbo as she was at the age of 30, given that Garbo has been dead for a number of years, is a resurrection of Garbo herself or instead a mere replica of her, whereas a reductionist would be able to regard this question as something to be determined by convention, in the unlikely event such a science fiction transformation were actually to take place.

In *The Further Fact View of Personal Identity*[15], I criticized this example of Parfit's as being unpersuasive because in fact it is quite easy to imagine a principled answer to the question of where the borderlines would be. All we need to do is to imagine a corresponding spectrum of cases where in each case the same percentage of cells are removed but are not replaced. At one end of the spectrum the scientists remove a few cells from Parfit's brain and body and don't replace them with any cells that are duplicates of ones from Garbo's brain and body as she was at 30 or with any other cells. In each succeeding case the scientists remove a slightly greater percentage of cells without replacing them. In the last case, at the far end of the spectrum, the scientists completely disassemble Parfit's brain and body, cell by cell, and don't replace any of the cells. Clearly, in the first few cases, where only a small percentage of cells are removed, the resulting person would be Parfit, i.e., Parfit would survive. It is also clear that in the case at the far end of the spectrum there is no resulting person at all, i.e., Parfit doesn't survive. The scientists have killed him. But it is also clear that somewhere in that spectrum of cases there would be a case where a critical percentage well short of 100% of cells being removed without being replaced would result in Parfit's death. It is perfectly plausible that the corresponding case in the original spectrum of cases, of cell removal with replacement by Garbo duplicate cells, would be the first case in which the resulting person would fail to be Parfit. That is, it would be the case in which the percentage of cells removed reached the critical point that would result in Parfit's death in the spectrum of cases of removal with no replacement. As for the first case in which the resulting person would be a duplicate of Garbo, we simply reverse the process, beginning with a case where there is a complete cell-by-cell replication of Garbo's brain and body as she was at age 30 and then proceeding through a series of cases where at first very small and then greater and greater percentages of the living replica's cells are removed without replacement, until we reach the case where the process kills her. The case just before that one would be the first case in Parfit's example where the resulting person would be a duplicate of Garbo. All the cases with percentages of cell destruction that correspond to those in which cell removal without replacement resulted in Parfit's death and the ones that correspond to those that resulted in Garbo's duplicate's death would be cases in which the resulting person is determinately neither Parfit nor a replica of Garbo.

So, I argued in that work, this example of Parfit's fails to undermine the non-reductionist intuitions that personal identity is what matters in survival and that it is not something that is a matter of degree and to be resolved, if at all, by mere stipulation or convention.

However, we can go further in the defense of a non-reductionist view than this rather minimalist criticism of Parfit's argument, by spelling out what the non-reductionist view implies. Just as important is the thought that the further fact, beyond any reductionist account, that personal identity consists in, is the first-person point of view from which each of us experiences the world. In every case in the spectrum of cases Parfit asks us to imagine, either Parfit would be experiencing the world from the point of view of the person who woke up after the scientists' experiment, in which case that person would be Parfit, or else Parfit would wake up in some other world where, at worst, he would remember a nightmare involving mad, unethical scientists; and the person who would wake up in this world would be someone else.

Is it conceivable that, even in the case where the scientists gradually remove all the cells in Parfit's brain and body and replace them with living, functioning cells that are exact duplicates of the ones that were in Garbo's brain and body as she was at age 30, with the result that a woman who is a perfect replica of Garbo at that age wakes up after the operation, has no memories or knowledge of Parfit, seems to remember what Garbo would have been able to remember, walks and talks and thinks like Garbo – is it conceivable that even in that case, that woman would actually be Parfit? I maintain that it is conceivable.

To see why, imagine that Parfit's invention of this spectrum of cases was inspired by a dream in which it seemed that he had agreed to take part in such an experiment. We can easily imagine that in the dream it would have seemed to him that there was some reason to do it, even though on reflection after waking up from the dream, he wouldn't be able to remember what it was. We can imagine that in the dream it seemed that he was being anaesthetized, asked to count backwards from 100, and that it seemed that he then found himself waking up after the operation, having strange memories, the belief that he was Greta Garbo, and the body and voice of a woman. Only then he wakes up again to find that he has not just awakened from the anesthesia within the dream but, he now realizes, that that first waking up was also a dream from which he has now awakened. If he told someone about this dream, he might say, "I dreamed that I was Greta Garbo, had her memories, her voice and body." Since we can imagine what it would be like for Parfit to have such a dream, we can imagine what it would be like for Parfit to survive as a duplicate of Garbo, experiencing the world by looking through her eyes, with her memories, her body, her feelings, her voice.

This shows that no matter what changes you undergo, you are still the one experiencing the world from a first-person perspective that no one else can occupy.

We can also imagine that Garbo herself, the original Garbo, is the one who wakes up in the body of the living replica the scientists have created, so that the replica is not a replica after all, but the resurrection of Garbo. In that case, Parfit wakes up in another world that will be just "the world" for him.

The first-person perspective, the fact that, out of all the people in the world, one is just this person and no other, is simply given to each one of us. Without it, no analysis of what personal identity consists in will enable us to understand what makes a particular person the one he or she is. I can imagine having a different body. I can imagine losing my memory and seeming to have a whole new set of memories. What I cannot imagine is going out of existence and being replaced by someone else, whether that person closely resembles me or doesn't resemble me at all – unless I imagine it as going out of existence while someone else takes over the role that I played in a world I have left behind, as I wake up into a new world. That is why the classic question uttered by someone who has just regained consciousness is not "Who am I?" but "Where am I?"

And here we have another reason why it is not only impossible for me to imagine myself as not existing but also impossible to imagine the world and other selves as not existing, for that question, "Where am I?" would always make sense, and it presupposes that there is an answer and an answerer. If someone were to propose that the answer might be "Nowhere" and that I might be the only answerer, my reply would be that this is not a real thinkable possibility, because the words "nowhere" and "I" would not have their usual meanings and it is hopelessly unclear what meanings they would have.

There are two senses to the question "Who am I?" One is the question of what makes me at one time the same person as I am at another time. This is the one I've been answering by arguing that it is simply given at each of those times that I am experiencing the world from this perspective and from no other. The other sense of "Who am I?" is a different question: "What am I like? What kind of person am I?" It isn't "Which person am I out of all the persons there are?" but rather, "Given that I am this person, what about this person? What kind of person do I turn out to be?"

Borges commented as follows on Heraclitus' saying, "No man steps twice into the same river."

Here we have the beginning of terror, because at first we think of the river as flowing on, of the drops of water being different. And then we are made to feel that *we* are the river, that we are as fugitive as the river.[16]

This is again Hume's idea that the subject of experience is just as unknowable and unnecessary as the hypothetical object that is something separate from all its observable properties. The terror would be that it now isn't a matter of worrying about suddenly going out of existence someday, but instead the worry has now become that I don't now exist and never have. But in order to realize that the river at one time doesn't consist of exactly the same waters as the river at another time, I myself must endure over that span of time from one thought to the next. It is all well and good to say, as Lichtenberg did, that Descartes was not justified in concluding "I am" from "I think," but was only justified in concluding that thinking was happening, as if to say, "It is thinking" in the same way we say "It is lightning" or "It is raining." But can anyone believe that thinking or experiencing of any type can occur from no point of view? To be objective is to take into account the fact that the world is experienced from other perspectives besides the one from which you experience it. It isn't to pretend that there is a kind of experience that is from no perspective.

But if I think about the other sense that can be given to the question "Who am I?"– that is, "What am I like?"– I find that I am not perturbed by some other philosopher's answer that I regard as unsatisfactory, nor am I terrified. I am just interested. Here maybe a reductionist account makes sense. I am the kind of person who has done the things that I have done and have had the thoughts and feelings that I have had. The kind of person I will be depends also on what I will do and think and feel. That is something that is partly under my control, whereas which person I am out of all the persons there are is just given and has never been under my control nor ever will be and doesn't change. That fact, however, doesn't support the claim that there is a simple unity of consciousness. I don't think anything I've written here is inconsistent with the observation made by H. H. Price:

> It appears that the unity of the human mind is a matter of degree and not a matter of all or none. And such unity as it has at any time is less stable than we ordinarily think... In all of us, I suggest, there is some degree of dissociation, the beginnings at least of a divided personality.[17]

Consciousness is a matter of degree, and our dreams should convince us that there is a lot more to us than our conscious waking lives would indicate. It is also possible that experience can come in a first-person plural version as well as in the more familiar first-person singular, as shown in Parfit's discussion of the divided minds created by surgeons treating severe epilepsy by disconnecting the two hemispheres of the brain.[18] This isn't so different from our ordinary usage of "we" when we think of ourselves as having a bond with each other despite our separateness, in that we recognize that we each have our own first-person perspective, and we each know what that is like. All I am saying is that the thought that there could be an experience that was from no particular point of view is one that I find myself incapable of understanding, and so I can't believe in the no-self doctrine of the Buddha, Hume, and Parfit. Each of us is a self.

That part is simple. What that self is like in each case, though, is a long and complicated story ever unfolding, as ancient as dust and as new as every morning.

Large parts of that story are lost to conscious memory, but life continues to well up from an inexhaustible source in dazzling yet soothing sensory brilliance. Why do I believe it is inexhaustible? Because the first-person perspective cannot imagine itself away.

Reason and faith don't conflict. I didn't create my first-person perspective. Experience just comes that way. Inductive reasoning doesn't support the belief that life is bounded on both ends by a state of being perfectly insensible, like Shakespeare's "brief candle" in the darkness. Imagining, or experiencing, perfect darkness and silence, one is there in that darkness and silence. One may lose consciousness, but one regains it.

It is a golden afternoon, and I bring this little book to a close. With each reader it will become something new.

Notes

1   from "On Learned Ignorance" in *Medieval Philosophy: From St. Augustine to Nicholas of Cusa*, p. 460

2   Edwards, Paul, ed., *Immortality*, p. 140

3   *A Treatise of Human Nature*, 2.3.3

4   quoted in *Immortality*, p. 140

5   *Who Knows? A Study of Religious Consciousness*, p. 14

6   quoted in *Immortality*, p. 139

7   *The Portable Nietzsche*, p. 52

8   *The Pneumatology of Matter*

9   *The Nag Hammadi Library*, p. 138

10 *Essays in the Philosophy of Religion*, p. 36

11 *Religion in the Making*, pp. 39-40

12 *A Treatise of Human Nature*, pp. 251-252

13 *A Treatise of Human Nature*, p. 636

14 *A Christian Natural Theology*, pp. 35-40

15 doctoral dissertation

16 *This Craft of Verse*, p. 26

17 *Philosophical Interactions with Parapsychology*, p. 214

18 *Reasons and Persons*, p. 245

Bibliography

Borges, Jorge Luis. *This Craft of Verse*. Cambridge, Massachusetts, and London, England: Harvard University Press, 2000.

Call, Jack. *God is a Symbol of Something True: Why you don't have to choose either a literal creator or a blind, indifferent universe.* Winchester, UK, and Washington, D.C., U.S.A.: Circle Books, 2009.

Cobb, John B., Jr. *A Christian Natural Theology, based on the thought of Alfred North Whitehead.* Louisville, Kentucky: Westminster John Knox Press, 2007.

De Senancour, Etienne Pivert. *Obermann*. Barnes, J. Anthony, trans. Baltimore: Noumena Press, 2010.

De Unamuno, Miguel. *Tragic Sense of Life.* Flitch, J.E. Crawford, trans. New York: Dover, 1954.

Dilley, Frank, and Price, H.H. *Philosophical Interactions with Parapsychology: The Major Writings of H.H. Price on Parapsychology and Survival.* Palgrave Macmillan, 1995.

Edwards, Paul, ed. *Immortality.* Amherst, New York: Prometheus Books, 1997.

Gunn, David. *The Pneumatology of Matter.* Winchester, UK, and Washington, D.C., U.S.A.: Iff Books, 2013.

Hartshorne, Charles. *The Divine Relativity: A Social Conception of God.* New Haven and London: Yale University Press, 1964.

Hume, David. *A Treatise of Human Nature.* Selby-Bigge, L.A., ed. Oxford: Oxford University Press, 1990.

Nietzsche, Friedrich. *The Portable Nietzsche.* Kaufman, Walter, ed. and trans. New York: The Viking Press, 1965.

Parfit, Derek. *Reasons and Persons.* Oxford: Oxford University Press, 1991.

Price, H.H. *Essays in the Philosophy of Religion.* Oxford: Oxford University Press, 2002.

Robinson, James M., ed. *The Nag Hammadi Library.* San Francisco:

HarperCollins, 1988.

Russell, Bertrand. *The Problems of Philosophy.* Oxford: Oxford University Press, 1959.

Schweitzer, Albert. *The Philosophy of Civilization.* New York: MacMillan, 1949.

Sidgwick, Henry. *The Methods of Ethics.* Indianapolis, Cambridge: Hackett Publishing, 1981.

Smullyan, Raymond M. *Who Knows? A Study of Religious Consciousness.* Bloomington and Indianapolis: Indiana University Press, 2003.

Whitehead, Alfred North. *Process and Reality.* New York: The Free Press, 1978.

—. *Religion in the Making.* Cambridge: Cambridge University Press, 2011.

Wippel, John F.; Wolter, Allan B.; Edwards, Paul; Popkin, Richard H., eds. *Medieval Philosophy: From St. Augustine to Nicholas of Cusa.* New York: The Free Press, 1969.

CHRISTIAN
ALTERNATIVE

Throughout the two thousand years of Christian tradition there
have been, and still are, groups and individuals that exist in the
margins and upon the edge of faith. But in Christianity's
contrapuntal history it has often been these outcasts and
pioneers that have forged contemporary orthodoxy out of
former radicalism as belief evolves to engage with and
encompass the ever-changing social and scientific realities. Real
faith lies not in the comfortable certainties of the Orthodox, but
somewhere in a half-glimpsed hinterland on the dirt track to
Emmaus, where the Death of God meets the Resurrection, where
the supernatural Christ meets the historical Jesus, and where the
revolution liberates both the oppressed and the oppressors.

Welcome to Christian Alternative... a space at the edge where
the light shines through.